What has happened in the first half of the twentieth century in the study and interpretation of the New Testament? What new discoveries, scholarly findings, and fresh insights have replaced old theories, discarded hypotheses, and popular conceptions? What established positions stand firm in clearer light?

The main purpose of this book is to set down the present state of New Testament studies and indicate to students of the Bible what the current trends are. But the author also mediates twentieth century findings for the average reader and reviews achievements of the past half century.

In a style marked by the eager vitality of an inquiring mind, Dr. Hunter surveys the field of new translations, and reports advances made in the last fifty years in the study of the Greek text, discussing the possibility of its Aramaic origin. He reviews the Synoptic Gospels, their origin and message, and considers Form Criticism in

New Testament studies. Dr. Hunter discusses the study of the life of Christ, singling out the best books of the last fifty years on this subject, and reviews the work done on the life and preaching of Paul. He considers all the New Testament books in turn, giving particular attention to the Gospel of John, and in concluding discusses the "theology of the New Testament," selecting for particular discussion six books that illustrate the direction of current trends.

Students and professors in colleges and seminaries will find this an illuminating and valuable companion book to more specialized studies of the New Testament. Its rich content and easy style will also appeal to the large group of ministers and laymen who like to keep well informed on recent discoveries and viewpoints.

Books by
Archibald M. Hunter
Published by The Westminster Press

Interpreting the New Testament, 1900-1950
The Work and Words of Jesus
Introducing the New Testament
The Message of the New Testament

INTERPRETING
the
NEW
TESTAMENT,

1900-1950, 225

Archibald M. Hunter

PHILADELPHIA

THE WESTMINSTER PRESS

First Published in Great Britain in 1951
by S.C.M. Press, Ltd.

Contents

❋

Preface

*

THIS book originated in the casual remark of a friend. We had been deploring the disadvantages of specialisation. A specialist has been defined as 'one who knows more and more about less and less.' Without entirely endorsing that cynical verdict, every writer in the theological field knows how hard it is to maintain even a bowing acquaintance with the work being done in other fields than his own. So continual is the stream of new books in his own subject that if he means to read all the important books appearing in his own field, he must sadly make up his mind that he cannot hope to read half of the important books appearing in other departments of theology. My friend, who is an Old Testament pundit, said: 'I am very interested in the New Testament too. But I simply have not time to keep abreast of what is being done in New Testament studies. Some one ought to write a little book, every two or three decades, setting down the present state of such studies and indicating current trends.'

This is the primary *raison d'être* of this book. But there are two others. One is the need for mediating the findings of the New Testament savants to the ordinary reader. Too often the writings of the experts moulder unread on the shelves of our libraries for lack of 'middle-men' to tell the ordinary reader what they are all about. So I have aimed to help not only my specialist friend but others, especially busy ministers who are too preoccupied with works of practical divinity to have leisure for keeping in close touch with the pundits.

A.D. 1950 is the third reason. Half of the twentieth century has now come and gone. It seems to me to be a good point in history to pause and do a bit of stocktaking: to review past achievements and to sketch present trends.

7

The book makes no claim to completeness. It is a survey, but a far from exhaustive one. It aims at providing a readable conspectus, not at chronicling everything that has been happening in New Testament studies in the last half century. Moreover, it has been written in the north-east corner of Great Britain. This means that British work on the New Testament is far better known to the writer than work being done in Germany, France, Switzerland, Scandinavia, or the U.S.A. For all sins of omission, all sins of insularity, and all sins of ignorance, he begs forgiveness.

For valued help in proof-reading, my cordial thanks are due to my friend, the Reverend H. M. Ricketts, B.D., minister at Craigiebuckler.

A. M. HUNTER

King's College
  Aberdeen University
February 1951

I

The Translation of the New Testament

❋

THE translation of 'the Word of God into the language of our time' is a dream that haunted Bede and King Alfred more than a millennium ago. Six centuries after Alfred Tyndale, being criticised by some pedant for indulging the same dream, boldly engaged: 'I will so bring it about that the boy at the plough's tail shall know more of the Bible than thou dost.' But this dream, this ambition, if old, is also modern. One of the more notable features of the first half of this twentieth century has been the number of attempts made to turn the New Testament into the language of our day. Hardly a decade has gone by without a fresh translator. At the turn of the century *The Twentieth Century New Testament* appeared (the translators' names were never divulged): and hard on its heels came the Weymouth version (1902). In 1913 Professor Moffatt made his now famous translation. In 1923 Professor Goodspeed did for American readers what Moffatt had done for people in this country. In 1938 came *The Book of Books*; and in 1946, again from the U.S.A., came the *Revised Standard Version*. Nor is this all. In 1935 Father Lattey completed for Roman Catholic readers a translation of the New Testament from the original Greek in *The Westminster Version of the Holy Scriptures*. In 1945 Monsignor Ronald Knox translated the Latin Vulgate into felicitous modern English. And at the present time a body of British scholars are setting their hands to yet another rendering which it is hoped may take its place in churches alongside the *Authorised Version*. If it be true that (in Coverdale's words) 'there cometh more understanding of the Scripture by sundry translations than by all the glosses of sophistical doctors' (a heavy blow

9

this at the commentators) we are suffering in this twentieth century from almost an embarrassment of hermeneutic riches.

I

If it is asked, What has caused this remarkable output? the answer can be put in one sentence. Not only can we understand New Testament Greek better, as we are in a position to make a better Greek text, but there is the demand of evangelism for a version which will clothe the Gospel in a language fully intelligible to the men of our day.

As proof of the great textual advance, we need here only point to the fact that the *Textus Receptus* underlying the Authorised Version is practically the text of Erasmus, who relied for the most part on a single twelfth-century manuscript; whereas (theoretically at any rate) the materials now at the disposal of the text-maker amount to nearly three thousand manuscripts or fragments thereof.[1] No less considerable have been the accessions to our linguistic and lexical knowledge of the New Testament. The Greek of the New Testament we now know to be not some special language of the Holy Ghost (as the old savant phrased it), but the common Greek of the world that was contemporary with Christ. And the papyri, so romantically exhumed from the sands of Egypt, have shed a wealth of light on both the grammar and vocabulary of evangelist and apostle.

But new needs as well as new knowledge have inspired these modern translators of the New Testament. Since the famous forty-seven did their work in 1611, nearly three and a half centuries have passed, and in that time our speech has so changed that the Authorised Version, for all the glories of its language, has grown more and more of a foreign tongue. The common man does not speak or properly understand the great accents of his Elizabethan ancestors. Were the Christian preacher or teacher concerned only with literary appreciation, he might rest content with the Authorised Version. But his task being what it is—to

[1] The statistics are: 170 papyrus MSS. and fragments; 200 uncial MSS. and fragments; 2,400 miniscules.

preach and teach the Word of God to a generation that is almost biblically illiterate and slowly lapsing into paganism—he demands, and rightly demands, a version of the New Testament that 'will clothe the Word of the Gospel in the vesture of our common speech' and come home with living power to men who do not understand, much less appreciate, the archaic splendours of Elizabethan prose.

To embody the new knowledge of text and language, and to meet this urgent evangelical need—these are the two chief purposes which have moved and inspired our twentieth century translators.

II

Of our modern translations, four—Weymouth's, Moffatt's, Goodspeed's and the *Revised Standard Version*—have been widely read and praised; and we propose to say something concerning each of them.

Dr. Weymouth, who was the Headmaster of Millhill School, brought to his task a fine classical equipment. He had made a text of the Greek Testament showing the text on which the majority of modern editors are agreed; and it was upon this 'Resultant Greek Testament' that he based his work. His classical training, his conviction that dignity of style demands a certain 'tinge of antiquity,' and the fact that he did his work before the lexical gains from the papyri were fully available all combine to give us a version which mediates between the manner of the Authorised Version and the demand for modernity. The result is a translation which is reverent, clear and accurate. If it seldom surprises us by brilliances of translation, it is free from all lapses from good taste. His rendering of the parable of the Good Samaritan will illustrate Weymouth's direct, dignified style:

A man was once on his way down from Jerusalem to Jericho when he fell among robbers, who after both stripping and beating him went away, leaving him half dead. Now a priest happened to be going along that road, and on seeing him passed by on the other side. In like manner a Levite also came to the place, and seeing him passed by on the other side. But a certain Samaritan, being on a journey, came where he lay, and seeing him was moved with pity. He went to him, and dressed his wounds with oil and wine and bound them up. Then placing him on his own mule he brought him to an inn, and took care of him. The next day he took out two shillings and gave them to the innkeeper.

'Take care of him,' he said, 'and whatever further expense you are put to, I will repay you at my next visit.'

'Which of those three seems to you to have acted like a neighbour to him who fell among the robbers?'

'The one who showed him pity,' he replied.

'Go,' said Jesus, 'and act in the same way' (Luke 10.30–37).

Much more modern, if less dignified, was the next rendering. Professor Moffatt, one of the polymaths of his time, stated his aim in the preface to his translation: 'My intention,' he wrote, 'has been to produce a version which will to some degree represent the gains of recent lexical research and also prove readable.' The text he used was that of Von Soden of Berlin, but he did not scruple to adopt emendations of the text (e.g. Rendel Harris's in I Pet. 1.12 and 3.19) or to transpose passages, especially in the Fourth Gospel, in order to get a better sequence. The whole thing was bold, modern and, in places, brilliant. It was like looking through a new window on an old landscape. It challenged by its modernity and infuriated all who believed in the inspiration of Elizabethan prose. The critics were not slow to criticise. Its colloquial style offended many who had been nurtured on the majestic cadences of the Authorised Version; a tendency to paraphrase irked the sticklers for accuracy; occasional Scotticisms (like 'factor' for 'land steward') annoyed those not fortunate enough to be born in Scotland; and the transpositions in the Fourth Gospel exasperated those who were not convinced that they were really necessary. But when the clouds of criticism had cleared away, it remained incontrovertibly clear that Dr. Moffatt had made the New Testament 'come alive' in modern speech.

Thus (to take some examples from Mark): Levi sits at 'the tax-office.' The family of Jesus say: 'He is out of his mind.' 'Is not this the joiner?' ask His fellow-townsmen in Nazareth. 'Get behind me, you Satan,' runs Peter's rebuking at Caesarea Philippi. When Jesus hands the broken loaf to His disciples in the Upper Room, it is with the words, 'Take this, it means my body.' And how modern the time of the Crucifixion sounds: 'It was nine in the morning when they crucified him.'

Yet no one who reads Moffatt's rendering of the Pauline Epistles can gainsay that they become human documents, astonishingly clear and alive, instinct with his whole vivid personality, in a way that they never do in the Authorised Version; and before such a passage as I Cor. 13.4–8 all criticism dies away upon his lips:

'Love is very patient, very kind. Love knows no jealousy; love makes no parade, gives itself no airs, is never rude, never selfish, never irritated, never resentful; love is never glad when others go wrong, love is gladdened by goodness, always slow to expose, always eager to believe the best, always hopeful, always patient.'

A decade after Moffatt's translation came Goodspeed's. Dr. Edgar J. Goodspeed of Chicago, doubtless thinking of Weymouth and Moffatt, essayed a translation 'free from expressions which, however familiar in England and Scotland, are strange to American ears.' The text he used was that of Westcott and Hort, and he sought to recapture in English 'something of the ease, boldness and unpretending vigor which mark the original Greek.' His translation, which reminds one of Moffatt's, has many merits. One likes, for example, his attention to what the grammarians call *Aktionsart* in the verb, and the resultant accurate translation of the Greek tenses. If Weymouth still hankered after something of the grace and dignity of the Authorised Version, Goodspeed will have modernity at all hazards. Thus he renders a famous sentence in the Prologue to the Fourth Gospel: 'So the Word became flesh and blood and lived for a while among us'; and, greatly daring, he makes the first words of the risen Lord to the women, 'Good morning!' Some examples from the Sermon on the Mount will show the quality of his version:

13

'Blessed are those who feel their spiritual need, for the Kingdom of heaven belongs to them' (Matt. 5.3).

'As long as heaven and earth endure, not one dotting of an *i* or crossing of a *t* will be dropped from the Law until it is all observed' (5.18).

'And if anyone wants to sue you for your shirt, let him have your coat too' (5.40).

'So do not worry about to-morrow, for to-morrow will have worries of its own' (6.34).

The last of our 'big four' versions differs from the other three in three respects. First, the *Revised Standard Version* is designed not only for private reading, but for ecclesiastical use. Second, it is the work not of an individual, but of a committee. And, third, it is a revision of a revision—since it revises the American Standard Version or transatlantic equivalent of our R.V.

Begun in 1930, it was published in 1946. The committee of nine scholars who made it included Moffatt and Goodspeed. Deciding on 'an eclectic text,' they arrived at one very like that of Westcott and Hort. Their aim was a version which, while conserving the style and manner of the Authorised Version, would be purged of its archaisms and errors.

The cordial welcome which its publication evoked on both sides of the Atlantic is proof that the selected nine scholars had done their work very well. This is a splendid version. It is clear. It is direct. It is accurate. It is eminently readable. And some of the beauty of the Authorised Version still haunts its cadences. To be sure, the experts have detected some surviving archaisms; disregard of tense-action is alleged in some places; perhaps, in certain passages, it has not shaken itself completely free of the word-for-word literalism which marred the Revised Version. But there is truth as well as enthusiasm in John Wick Bowman's verdict: 'By far the best translation of the Christian scriptures ever made in the English language.' A few quotations made almost at random will reveal the force and felicity of the R.S.V.:

'*She has done a beautiful thing to me*' (Mark 14.6).

'*In my Father's house are many rooms*' (John 14.2).

'*We know that in everything God works for good with those who love him*' (Romans 8.28).

'*Knowledge puffs up, but love builds up*' (I Cor. 8.1).

'*Our commonwealth is in heaven*' (Phil. 3.20).

III

One might have supposed that those who desired a modern translation of the New Testament for all occasions would have accepted the *Revised Standard Version* as the answer to their prayers. But for a little group in Scotland it was not modern enough and suffered from the disadvantage of being a twentieth-century revision of a seventeenth century classic. Accordingly, in 1946, the General Assembly of the Church of Scotland approved a plan for a new translation of the Bible in the language of to-day which might be authorised for use in churches. The co-operation of the other Churches in Britain was sought and obtained, and plans were made for translation and publication, by a Joint Committee.

The work has now begun, and it may be of interest to summarise the method of procedure which is proposed.

First, two advisory panels for the Old and New Testaments respectively were created, and invitations to join these were sent out to leading British Biblical scholars. These panels (we learn) framed the principles of the work and chose the translators; five for the Old Testament and three for the New. When the chosen eight have completed their drafts, they will be submitted for the criticism of the panels. Finally, before the text is sent off to the Churches' Joint Committee for the whole project, it will be 'vetted' by certain eminent English men of letters. The publication of the new translation has been entrusted to the Oxford and Cambridge University Presses, who will hold the copyright and undertake all the editorial and publication expenses.

It is hardly necessary to say that the translators are embarked on a delicate and difficult task. There will always be those who, 'thirled' to the language of the Authorised Version, will say, 'The old is better.' Such conservatism apart, the translation of an ancient tongue into the words and idioms of to-day is a task that bristles with difficulties. To begin with, our translators have to make the best text possible, utilising all the resources of modern textual criticism. This done, they have to translate it accurately (yet in the light of our knowledge of the *Koine*, not over-subtly), paying attention to tenses, especially the Greek aorist, and doing what they can to render words like δικαιοσύνη and ἱλαστήριον into their nearest English equivalents. Theirs must be a modern rendering, shorn of all obsolete or obsolescent terms; yet they must guard against too flagrant colloquialisms. They must not render too freely, or they will have the precisians on their top. Or too literally and word-for-word, or the literary men will convict them of 'translation English.' Sometimes, *feliciter audax,* the translator will hit the mark, and achieve in English the precise *nuance* of the Greek phrase; oftener the best that he can hope to do is to score a near miss. ὑποκριτής may go neatly into English as 'humbug,' but what single English verb will do duty for σκανδαλίζω? And he must keep it up, this high level of excellence, not merely in single phrases or verses, but through whole books. He must never dream that he will please everybody; and in the end, when he has done his task, he will be well aware that something of the original has evaporated in the process of translation, and that failure, albeit a glorious one, is the lot appointed him.

Nevertheless, whatever the hazards and difficulties, it is a high and urgent emprise on which our latest translators are embarked —this task of translating the lively oracles of God into the speech of our time.

II

The Text of the New Testament

※

STRICTLY speaking, this chapter should have come before the last one. Before you can translate the New Testament, you must make a proper text of it. Textual criticism may be only a humble handmaid to the Queen of the sciences, but we cannot dispense with her services. Unless she do her work well and truly, we cannot begin to build any sort of secure edifice, theological or otherwise.

The textual critic is a man with a great ideal before him. It is nothing less than to lay bare the actual Greek which the Evangelists, Paul and the other Apostolic men wrote down on papyrus somewhere between A.D. 50 and 150. His materials are the thousands of surviving New Testament manuscripts—papyrus fragments from the sands of Egypt (two at least going back to the second century), stately vellum codices in uncial characters from the fourth century on, minuscules from the tenth century written in cursive script, early versions of the New Testament in Latin, Syriac, Coptic, etc., and quotations of the New Testament in the early Fathers of the Church from Marcion to Augustine. Into the text on which he works have crept errors innumerable—not only conscious alterations, but undesigned errors of sight, hearing and memory committed by the scribes who copied the sacred text for almost fourteen hundred years, till printing was invented. These it is his business to discover, explain, remove. Manuscript has to be compared with manuscript to discover its family history, so that its worth may be appraised. Variant readings are the textual critic's stock in trade; collation his business; palaeography in its many aspects his art and science; and his hope

17

is that at the end of his day he may have cleared one little patch of a wide ground so that his successors may the better go forward towards the unrealised ideal—a *Graeca Veritas* sans spot or wrinkle, a text of the Greek New Testament from which, so far as human skill can compass it, all errors of transcription have been removed.

How far have we progressed towards that ideal in the last fifty years? For a proper answer, we must go back not fifty but seventy years—to be precise, to 1881.

I

1881 was an *annus mirabilis* in the study of the text. In that year the Revised Version of the New Testament was published; but —more important for our purpose—it was the year in which B. F. Westcott (later Bishop of Durham) and F. J. A. Hort (Hulsean Professor of Divinity in Cambridge University) set the seal on twenty-eight years' work on the text by producing their great critical edition of the Greek New Testament. That edition marked an epoch in textual science whose characteristic sign is the two letters, fitly run together, WH. The text which they produced and the theory which underlies it have formed the basis for all later study and provided a battleground over which many learned men have fought.

Westcott and Hort were not pioneers: their work crowned the labours of many scholars, English and German, over three hundred years: Erasmus and Stephanus and Beza; Walton, Fell (hero of a famous stanza) and Mill; Richard Bentley, the renowned classical scholar; Wettstein of Basel and Bengel of Tübingen (who first divided the MSS. into families); Griesbach, Lachmann, Tregelles, and Tischendorf who discovered more Biblical MSS. than any other man and produced no less than eight editions of the Greek New Testament. Into the labours of these Westcott and Hort entered.

Let us sum up the conclusions to which they came, as expounded for us by Hort.

Confronted with corruption in the text, how are we to pro-

ceed? The first step is to apply the tests called 'critical probabilities.' We ask, Which reading gives the better sense? (intrinsic
probability). Then we ask, Which of two variant readings is the
likelier to have produced the other? (This is called 'transcriptional
probability.') Occasionally these two tests may produce the same
answer; oftener we find ourselves up against a clash of critical
probabilities. We must go further.

The next step is to note which MSS. provide superior readings.
This helps us to a comparative estimate of documents. With this
estimate as guide, we may then, when in doubt, follow the MSS.
usually found to be superior. But, next, it will become possible
to classify the MSS. in groups, or families, by noting which of
them are commonly found supporting certain variant readings.
This will imply descent from some common ancestor now lost,
and so carry us back to a time much earlier than our MSS.

So the WH theory ran; and when it was worked out, they
found four families among the MSS.: Syrian, Neutral, Alexandrian and Western.

First, and least important, was a great mass of MSS. whose
'conflate' (or mixed) readings suggested they were the result of a
revision made in the fourth century, probably at Syrian Antioch.
For the purpose of getting back to the original text, these Syrian
MSS. could be ignored.

Next came a few MSS. headed by B (Codex Vaticanus) and
S (Codex Sinaiticus) which, because they seemed to show least
evidence of corruption, they called Neutral, i.e. pure.

The third group was represented by C (Codex Ephraemi) and
L (Codex Regius). Akin to the Neutral family, it possessed certain
scholarly refinements which suggested an origin in Alexandria—
hence the name.

Last came a group, headed by D (Codex Bezae) and supported
by the Old Latin Version, which had many striking variants in
Luke and Acts. This, because of its Latin attestation, they called
Western.

But this choice among four is really (said WH) a choice
between two. For we can put aside the Syrian MSS. as late and

impure; and the Alexandrian is so like the Neutral as to look like a sub-family. How then are we to decide between the Neutral and the Western texts? Faced with the claims of the Western, we cannot invoke the evidence of the Fathers against it (as in the case of the Syrian text); for nearly all the early Fathers have some Western readings. The test of intrinsic probability must decide the issue. So WH, after bidding us see in the Western variants a licentious handling of the text by some early scribes, invite us to pin our faith to the Neutral family, especially B. But we must qualify this judgment in one direction—that of Western non-interpolations. If the Western text omits anything, e.g. the second mention of the Cup in Luke 22.19f., the omission is likely to be primitive, for the genius of the Western text is all towards addition.

Roughly, then, WH's advice about the text was this: 'With the one exception just mentioned, beware of the Western text. Follow the Neutral, and unless it is clearly a scribal error, never think it safe to reject the testimony of B.' We shall presently consider how the WH theory looks after seventy years of criticism. Meanwhile, let us only note that though their theory provoked immediate and fiery opposition from defenders of the Received Text like Dean Burgon, at the end of the century most scholars had accepted the WH view. In one respect only did some hesitate—WH's judgment on the Western text. Loth to regard B as a second infallible voice speaking from the Vatican, they pleaded for more consideration for the Western text.

II

What advances have we made since 1881? If we had to characterise the seventy years in one sentence, picking out the 'high lights,' the answer would run something like this. 1881-1950 is the record of a great 'find' (the Chester Beatty Papyri), an ill-starred edition (Von Soden's), and an exciting textual discovery (the Caesarean text). We shall start with the 'finds.'

Our first date is 1892, the year in which Mrs. Lewis, one of the famous twin sisters, discovered the Sinaitic palimpsest of the

Gospels. This MS. (with the Curetonian Syriac) shows us the text of the Gospels current in the Church at Edessa at the beginning of the third century A.D. In 1906 Charles L. Freer of the U.S.A. bought from an Arab dealer in Cairo a fifth-century MS. of the Gospels with a mixed text of great interest, now known as W (Codex Washingtonianus). Seven years later saw the publication of the Koridethi Gospels, an eighth-century MS. once in the Koridethi Monastery on the Black Sea, and now denominated Θ.

But the most exciting additions to our manuscript wealth in the last fifty years have been New Testament papyri from the sands of Egypt. Until their discovery the time-gap between our earliest MSS. and the original text was nearly three hundred years. We may mention first two tiny papyrus fragments. One (published in 1935) belonging to the second century, was a piece of an unknown gospel and contained four episodes in the life of Jesus. The other, also published in 1935, contained five verses of John 18. This is the earliest bit of the New Testament in existence. The experts judge its date to be anywhere between A.D. 95 and 125. Its discovery, not in Asia Minor (the probable home of the Fourth Gospel), but in middle Egypt, makes all dating of the Gospel after A.D. 100 highly improbable. But by far the most important MS. discovery since Tischendorf unearthed Codex Sinaiticus has been the finding of the Chester Beatty Papyri in 1931. This collection of papyrus, called after its owner, includes three codices of the New Testament. The first, which is very imperfect, has about one-seventh of what was once a complete codex of the Gospels and Acts. The second has most of the Pauline Epistles, except the Pastorals. The third contains the middle portion of Revelation. These codices, called P45, P46, and P47 respectively, all belong to the third century, and the Pauline one may be as early as A.D. 200. Their discovery means that we have now MSS. of a great part of the New Testament not much more than a hundred years later than the original writings. This is a gain of very considerable importance.

The finding of early MSS. is, however, only the first step;

the next is to study their text, and see what help they contribute towards the making of a better critical edition of the New Testament.

In the first decade of the twentieth century, therefore, Von Soden of Berlin set himself the task of improving on Tischendorf and Westcott and Hort. His aim was not merely to produce a new edition, but to provide a complete list of variant readings and a new theory of the text. When his edition appeared in 1913, however, it greatly disappointed the scholars. His new method of denominating and numbering the MSS. was intolerably complicated; and his textual theory, which classified the MSS. into three groups called I (Jerusalem), H (Hesychian) and K (Koine), puzzled by its nomenclature and did not please by its grouping. The experts adjudged Von Soden to have overrated the bad influence of Tatian's *Diatessaron* on the early Greek text, and to have underrated the importance of the Versions. In the end, the edition which had promised so richly, which Moffatt used in making his translation, and which showed great erudition, proved to be a failure. The 'new Tischendorf' was still to make.

What changes had been coming over textual theory all this time?

The first reaction to the WH theory was a taking-up of critical cudgels on behalf of the Western text. Was it fair (it was asked) to dismiss all these striking variants of the Western text (especially in Luke-Acts) as the work of licentious scribes? Foremost among the champions of Codex Bezae was Rendel Harris. Hort had used the evidence of the early Fathers to condemn the Syrian type of text. If it was a question of patristic evidence, the Western text, which occurs in Justin and Tertullian, had even better claims than the Neutral. So a battle raged round the claims of the Western text for the next few decades, and as late as 1933 A. C. Clark of Oxford was found vigorously supporting the Western text against the Neutral. A book of this kind cannot go into the pros and cons; but it may be said briefly that fuller discussion has tended to weaken rather than confirm the claims made for the Western text.

We must now turn aside to describe the discovery of the new type of text called 'Caesarean.' The story reads like a first-class piece of detection in which several textual sleuths played notable parts. It begins away back in 1868, when Ferrar of Dublin picked out four minuscule MSS. (headed by 13) as forming a single group marked by striking variants (e.g. the transference of John 7.53–8.11 to a position after Luke 21.38). Then, in 1902, Kirsopp Lake identified another group of minuscules (headed by 1) with like peculiarities. When, in 1913, the Koridethi Gospels appeared, Mark was found to show the same type of text, a text that could hardly be fitted into WH's scheme. Finally, in 1924, B. H. Streeter showed that all these MSS. made up one family, and that readings of this kind occurred in Origen's writings during the last period of his life, when he had moved from Alexandria to Caesarea (231–240). Hence he called it 'Caesarean.' (When the text of Mark in P45 was studied, the experts again traced these Caesarean marks.) In all this, of course, we are moving, however rashly, in the rarefied realms of higher scholarship where only a very few experts have the right to speak with authority; but what they seem to be reporting to us is the isolation of a new family of MSS. and a new type of text—a text midway between the Neutral and the Western. If they are right —and the whole matter is still *sub judice*—this too is a conclusion of much importance.

III

We have fetched a wide compass, and it is now time to hark back to our starting-point: How does the WH theory stand to-day? Of the four families, one has disappeared. The so-called Alexandrian has been absorbed in the Neutral; and indeed nowadays the Neutral is sometimes called the Alexandrian, since Alexandria was its probable place of origin. Save for accessions to its number, the Syrian family remains as it was. Hort's judgment on it stands unaltered. Not in this family's keeping, however numerous its members, is the secret of the true text.

The Western text is still the storm-centre in textual criticism.

But its range has been narrowed; for it is nowadays agreed that the core of this text must be sought in D and the Old Latin version. How to appraise the value of its variants is still the problem. If J. H. Ropes is sure that the Western text 'is inferior to the text found in the Old Uncials, or even in the mass of later manuscripts,' others[1] in our time have pointed to the Aramaisms in its readings as evidence of its primitive character. The end of the controversy is not yet in sight. But after seventy years it is clear enough that we must treat this text with more respect than it received at the hands of WH.

The new-found Caesarean text is, of course, still under investigation. Its best representatives are Θ, families 1 and 13, W and P45. Possibly 'Caesarean' may be a misnomer after all, for Lake has argued (against Streeter) that Egypt was its home. As a text (says Kenyon) it stands between B and D. Lacking the extravagances of D, it shares many of its minor variants; but in the major variants it is with B.

We come lastly to the Neutral text and Codex Vaticanus in particular. Nobody nowadays is quite so sure as Hort that this great MS. has escaped the attentions of the reviser. But if it has been edited, it has been well edited, as indeed we should expect if it originated in Alexandria.

What, then, is our general conclusion? No single type of text may claim to be 'neutral' in the sense of everywhere preserving the Greek verity; but Westcott and Hort did not greatly err. Most scholars, if challenged, would still award the palm to that text which finds its best representatives in B and S, 33 ('the Queen of the cursives') and the Coptic Versions.

Tasks there are in plenty still awaiting those prepared to undertake the unspectacular work of textual criticism. Many new materials lie to hand. The Caesarean text has yet to be fully investigated. But our last word must be of a very important project in which scholars on both sides of the Atlantic are now engaged. It is none other than the production of 'the new Tischendorf' or, to speak more exactly, the new Oxford Edition

[1] E.g. M. Black.

of the Greek New Testament. Work on it began in the 'thirties: a committee was formed with the late Bishop Headlam as chairman and the Rev. S. C. E. Legg as editor. The aim is to print the WH text[1] and beneath it a list of variants from all the important MSS., including the Chester Beatty Papyri. Thus far, Mark and Matthew have appeared. The work, interrupted by World War II, has now been resumed in earnest; and a joint committee of American and British scholars are now addressing themselves to this immense task. When it is completed, New Testament scholars will be equipped with an up-to-date and invaluable tool for reconstructing the text of the New Testament—an *apparatus criticus* which will truly reflect the many and magnificent discoveries of Biblical manuscripts in our time.

[1] The next book to be done is Luke. It has been decided that in future the *Textus Receptus*, not the WH text, shall be printed.

III

Aramaic Origins

*

THAT the Incarnation meant, among other things, a Jew of the first century speaking Aramaic and addressing God as *Abba* is common knowledge. That Aramaic is a Semitic tongue resembling Hebrew and surviving in some chapters of Daniel and Ezra is also well known. But that Aramaic was one of the great and ancient languages of the East in the centuries before Christ—a sort of *lingua franca* from the Euphrates to the Nile—is now becoming clear.

It was in one of the many dialects of this language—Palestinian Aramaic—that Jesus preached, and taught His disciples, and said His prayers. Hebrew, the language of the sacred scriptures, remained the learned language of the rabbis; but among the people of the land, whose ancestors had learned it during and after the Exile, Aramaic was the common tongue. Greek was the language of the Hellenised classes, and Jesus no doubt knew something of it. Latin was the language of the army of occupation, and perhaps Jesus had a few words of it. (He would understand the demoniac when he said, 'We are *legion*.') But beyond doubt it was in Palestinian Aramaic that John the Baptist called Israel to repentance and, when 'the time was fulfilled,' that Jesus came preaching the Kingdom of God.

What remains of this language do we possess? Literary Aramaic writings contemporary with the Gospels do not exist, or have not been found. What Aramaic remains we have belong to before the second century B.C. or after the second century A.D. And the question which of these remains is most like the Aramaic spoken by Jesus is greatly exercising our Semitic savants today.

Fifty years ago, when Dalman of Germany was our great authority, the belief was that the Aramaic of the Targums (i.e. Aramaic paraphrases of scripture) of Onkelos and Jonathan provided the best clue to Jesus' mother-tongue. Our latest authorities, Paul Kahle and Matthew Black, believe, however, that the nearest parallel is to be found in a Palestinian Pentateuch recently unearthed in the Cairo Geniza (the lumber-house of the synagogue) as well as in some Samaritan Aramaic and Christian Syriac remains. But this is to anticipate.... Let us go back to the basic problem.

I

Our four Gospels are written in Greek—'common Greek,' as it is called, the simplified vernacular Greek which Alexander the Great and his armies had done so much to make the international language of the Graeco-Roman world. But the Greek of the Gospels is not simply 'common Greek'—the Greek which we can parallel in the thousands of papyri exhumed during the last fifty or sixty years from the sands at Oxyrhynchus and other places in Upper Egypt. It is Semitised Greek. Behind the Greek of the Gospels we detect the mind, the mode of speech, the idioms of men who did their thinking in Semitic ways, in Aramaic. (Even when we repeat in English—which translates Greek—the words of the Lord's Prayer, 'Forgive us our *debts*, as we forgive our debtors,' we are unconsciously perpetuating an Aramaic idiom; for it is not in Greek, or even in Hebrew, but in Aramaic that sin is conceived in terms of debt.)[1] In much of the Gospels, especially the sayings of Jesus, we can trace the forms of Semitic poetry, the word-order, asyndeton, parataxis, proleptic pronouns, prepositional usages, etc., which point unmistakably to the original Aramaic background of the Gospels. And sometimes when the Greek puzzles us, and we think back into what may have been the original Aramaic, we seem to detect what looks like a mistranslation.

Our Gospels, though they wear a Greek dress, are therefore in

[1] M. Black in *The Expository Times*, April, 1948, 171.

some sense translations from Aramaic. But in what sense? Are they straight translations from original Aramaic documents? Or do they depend on sources which were originally written down in Aramaic? Or are they translations only in the sense that the sayings of Jesus and the stories about Him were first formulated in Aramaic, whether or no they were ever committed to writing in that tongue?

These questions pose the Aramaic problem. On many aspects of it the experts (alas! a dwindling number) still disagree. But in the last fifty years several noted scholars have made contributions of high value to the debate.

II

If we single out the work of three scholars, we shall get a broad idea of the issues under discussion, the views held, and the progress made.

The three books we choose are:

The Words of Jesus, by Gustaf Dalman (Eng. Tr., 1902).
The Four Gospels, by C. C. Torrey (1933).
An Aramaic Approach to the Gospels and Acts, by M. Black (1946).

Gustaf Dalman, who spent much of his life in Palestine, did perhaps more than any other to interest the ordinary student in Aramaic origins. He found the hypothesis of an Aramaic original for the Synoptic tradition highly probable; but, unable to verify it further, he set himself to study the main ideas in our Lord's teaching in the light of their Aramaic background. Let us take 'the Kingdom of God' as an example of the new light which his studies provided. To a generation accustomed to interpret the Kingdom in terms of evolution and progress, it was salutary to have Dalman's reminder that the Aramaic word which Jesus used, *malkutha,* means 'sovereignty' and that the 'sovereignty of God' which Jesus proclaimed was something very different from a nineteenth-century Christian dream of Utopia. We have to do with an activity of God—God's sovereign power in action—not with an achievement of man. In all his work Dalman assumed that the nearest approach to the Aramaic which Jesus spoke was that found in the Targums of Onkelos and Jonathan on the Pentateuch and the Prophets. There might be Aramaic sources underlying our Gospels; but no proof was possible. The one entirely certain fact was that Jesus spoke in Aramaic to His disciples. This we may call 'the minimal theory' of Aramaic influence in the Gospels.

Thirty years later we had a 'maximal' one. In 1933 Professor C. C. Torrey of Yale, in his *Four Gospels*, boldly claimed that all four Gospels were translations of Aramaic documents and dated all of them earlier than A.D. 60. Eleven years before, Burney of Oxford (in a book which we shall have to notice later) had tried to prove the Fourth Gospel to be the translation of an Aramaic original, laying great weight on alleged mistranslations. Torrey out-Burneyed Burney. Reading his book, one gets the impression that every difficulty in the Greek text must be set down as a mistranslation from the Aramaic. 'All of his proposed emendations are ingenious,' observes E. F. Scott, 'and some of them exceedingly happy. Yet one is left almost always with the feeling that the text is at least equally intelligible as it stands.' Let us take Matt. 5.48 as an example. 'Ye therefore shall be perfect [τέλειοι],' says Jesus to His disciples, 'as your heavenly Father is perfect.' Torrey dismisses this call to perfection as 'mere nonsense.' Nothing leads up to it: Jesus does not expect his disciples to equal God's perfection. But go back to the underlying Aramaic, and all becomes clear. The Aramaic behind 'perfect' was *g'mar*. 'The explanation of the false rendering lies, very obviously, in the fact that the form of *g'mar* (certainly used here) was active and not passive in signification.' What Jesus really said was 'Be all-including,' or, as we might render it, 'Be catholic, as your heavenly Father is catholic.' This explanation is undoubtedly attractive: it fits in perfectly with the nearby conception of God who 'maketh his sun to rise on the evil and the good, and sendeth rain on the just and on the unjust.' But before we can finally accept it, we must be sure of two things: (*a*) that we can make nothing of the Greek text before us; and (*b*) that there is chapter and verse in contemporary Aramaic for this meaning of *g'mar*. Thus, in example after example, Torrey finds mistranslations and by deft guessing at the original Aramaic smooths difficulties away. Often he may well be right, but we constantly have the uneasy suspicion that he is too prone to blame the translator into Greek for any difficulties in the text. Torrey was not unaware that he had laid himself open to the charge of 'uncertain renderings' and 'unwarranted conclusions,' but he stoutly asserted the truth of his main thesis. 'The main fact of translated Gospels is quite certain,' he wrote, 'and so also is the early date of the four great documents of Christian truth. Later research will improve the demonstration which here is incomplete.'

The event has proved Torrey too sanguine. Later research has hardly confirmed his prophecy. In his very able book published in 1946 Dr. Matthew Black finds many of Torrey's conjectures open to grave objection, and he obviously regards his main thesis as unproved. His own approach is by way of an examination of the Aramaic traits in the syntax, grammar and vocabulary of the Gospels. Carefully he studies the style and structure of the Gospel sentences for traces of Aramaic idiom. And in two directions he breaks new ground. To begin with, Dalman is wrong in supposing the Targums of Onkelos and Jonathan to be our best clues to Jesus' mother-tongue. The Targum Aramaic is 'Hebraised,' and has been influenced by Babylonian Aramaic. His other conclusion links up linguistics with textual criticism; for he holds that the D (or Western) text of the Gospels, stained as it is with Aramaisms, takes us nearer to the original text than the SB (or Neutral) text preferred by most. On the main question, he finds one conclusion only established—that an Aramaic sayings-source underlies the Synoptic tradition. We cannot be sure whether it was written or oral. Many have held that the sayings-source Q existed originally in Aramaic. Dr. Black does not deny this, but he thinks it equally arguable that Mark had access to an Aramaic sayings-source, for he finds Mark's narrative the most Semitic among the Gospels. As for the Fourth Gospel, he thinks that the sayings of Jesus there may also depend on some Aramaic source, though, as we have them, they have been heavily 'targumised.'

How is the ordinary student who knows no Aramaic to think of the whole problem? Enough has been said to warn him against unreserved acceptance of Torrey's claim. It is highly improbable that our Four Gospels are straight translations of Aramaic originals. Somewhere between this 'maximal' theory and the 'minimal' one the truth must lie. T. W. Manson's conclusion will commend itself to many. 'The only case in which one may feel fairly confident that a written Aramaic source lies behind the Gospels is that of the document Q.'[1] The Aramaisms in Mark may all be explicable on the theory that Mark was a man who wrote in Greek, but thought in Aramaic. One thing is clear: recognition of the Aramaic element in the Gospels has been steadily growing in the last fifty years.

III

Perhaps the most exciting part of all this quest for Aramaic is the attempt to feel one's way beneath the Greek to the original Aramaic, keeping a weather-eye open for mistranslations. Obviously, there is plenty of scope here for brilliant guessing. We must guard against the temptation to reject Greek which, though well attested in the MSS., is theologically inconvenient and to prefer Aramaic which, while theologically attractive, is pure conjecture. Dr. Black insists that before we accept any reconstructions we must make two demands: (*a*) that the mistranslation must be credible; and (*b*) that the conjectured Aramaic must be possible. Here, therefore, in the last resort, we are in the hands of the experts. Nevertheless, when all tests have been applied, there remain some conjectures which have high probability on their side; and, to conclude this chapter, we propose to mention six of them.

An old one concerns Matt. 7.6:

> *Give not that which is holy unto the dogs,*
> *Neither cast your pearls before the swine.*

[1] *Expository Times*, October, 1935.

Holy does not make a very good parallel to *pearls*. Possibly the Greek ἅγιον (*kadosh*) mistranslates the Aramaic *kedasha,* Hebrew *nezem*: 'a ring,' generally of gold. Since the rabbis sometimes called the Law *nezem,* and its precepts 'pearls,' what Jesus really said may have been:

> *Give not a (costly) ring to dogs,*
> *Neither cast your pearls before swine.*

Our second example brings in the Western text as well as Aramaic to provide a solution. It is notorious that the Greek MSS. vary greatly in Mark 4.8, 20 between the prepositions εἰς and ἐν. *Codex Bezae,* however, for prepositions has numerals: ἓν ἑξήκοντα καὶ ἓν ἑκατόν. This may well be an original Aramaism; for Aramaic, as Dan. 3.9 shows, uses the numeral *har* 'one' with other numerals to form the multiplicative. Probably therefore in all three cases in Mark we should read ἓν and translate: 'thirty-fold, sixty-fold and a hundred-fold.'

In the story of the Centurion's Servant the officer says: 'I am a man under authority (ὑπὸ ἐξουσίαν), having under myself soldiers: and I say to this one, Go and he goeth; and to another, Come, and he cometh' (Matt. 8.9: Luke 7.8).

There is a difficulty here. After saying that he is one who receives orders, the Centurion describes himself as one who gives orders. All would have been clear if he had said, 'I am one representing authority, etc.' The offence lies in the Greek preposition ὑπό. But light dawns when we remember that the corresponding Aramaic preposition *tehoth* is ambiguous. It may mean either 'under' or 'in place of.' Are we not then justified in guessing that what the Centurion really said was: 'I am a man in place of, i.e. representing, authority, etc.'?

Consider, next, the puzzling 'give for alms' of Luke 11.41 with its parallel in Matt. 23.26. Matthew has: 'Cleanse first the inside of the cup and of the platter, that the outside thereof may become clean also.' Luke's version runs: 'Give for alms those things which are within, and behold, all things are clean unto you.' Years ago Wellhausen, stumped by Luke's 'give for alms,' pointed out the likeness between the Aramaic for 'cleanse' (*dakki*) and for 'give for alms' (*zakki*) and suggested that Luke wrongly read as 'give for alms' the Aramaic rightly rendered by Matthew 'cleanse.' The verse in Luke will then mean: 'Cleanse the inside [i.e. the heart], and then all is pure for you.' Few conjectures are more probable than this.

Now look at the Q passage Luke 11.48: Matt. 23.31. Luke has: 'For they killed them, and ye build.' For 'ye build' Matthew has: 'Ye are the children [of those who killed the prophets].' When we remember that the Aramaic for Luke's phrase is *banin* and for Matthew's *benin,* it looks as if Luke has mistranslated and that we should render (with Torrey): 'Ye are their children.'

In our last example, again from Q (Luke 12.46: Matt. 24.51), we are told that the master of the unfaithful slave 'will cut him in pieces and appoint his portion with the unfaithful.' There is something wrong here. What is the sense of setting a man among the unfaithful when he has already been dismembered? The solution may lie in the fact that while the Hebrew verb *nittach* does mean 'cut in pieces,' the corresponding Aramaic verb means 'separate.' If so, we may render: 'He will separate him [from the rest] and appoint his portion with the unfaithful.'

On which mitigatory note we may end our study of Aramaic origins.

IV

The Synoptic Gospels

✳

THE aim of all Gospel study—indeed, of all New Testament study—is to find out the truth about Jesus Christ. The simple believer may rest content with the four Gospels in the King James Version, asking no questions; but any man who aspires to add to his faith knowledge, asks like Oliver Twist for more. He wants to know, if possible, who wrote the Gospels, and when, and where, and why. He wishes also to know what sources lay before our evangelists when they wrote. And if it were possible, he would fain learn what account of Jesus and his message was current among Christians before any account was written down.

It is a tall demand, and one that in the nature of the case we can never completely satisfy. Our Gospel records are fragmentary, our science is inadequate, and to push past documents into the hinterland of oral tradition is a hard and hazardous task. Yet there is no case for despair; for the scepticism which talks of 'the Christ myth' or tells us that the Gospels can only give us 'the whisper of Jesus' voice' can be put aside at once. If we do not know all, we know much, and the New Testament study of the last fifty years can answer many of our questions.

I

We may start on a positive note. Modern scholarship can lay before us the outline of the apostolic Gospel which was proclaimed before any of our Gospels were written down. It was neither a new philosophy, nor an improved code of ethics, nor a revolutionary political programme. It was (to use the technical Greek word) a *kerygma*—a proclamation of God's Good News

34

uttered to men in Jesus Christ. Good News, but not absolutely new News, for as the apostolic preachers never tired of insisting, this Good News was really the fulfilment of the promises and prophecies of God in the Old Testament. 'The Good News of God,' says Paul, 'was promised beforehand through His prophets in the holy scriptures,' and it concerns 'His Son born of the seed of David according to the flesh' (Rom. 1.2f.).

Thanks to C. H. Dodd and others, we are able to recover the outline of the *kerygma*.[1] We have two main sources of information. To begin with, we can use those passages in St. Paul's letters where he is obviously reproducing the common doctrine of the primitive Church—for example, Rom. 1.2f. and 10.9 and I Cor. 11.23ff. and 15.3ff. (these two latter passages being expressly described by Paul as part of what he had 'received'). The early sermons in Acts form our second source. Time was when the critics dismissed these as the free compositions of St. Luke. Closer study of them has compelled us to revise our estimate. Nowadays, though few would claim them as verbatim reports of what Peter said, most scholars hold that they preserve very early Christian tradition, a tradition that has all the marks of having been once in Aramaic. The clearest example of all is the speech in Acts 10.36-43.

By comparing these two sources, we can arrive, with some certainty, at the substance of the earliest apostolic message. It ran somewhat as follows:

The prophecies are fulfilled, and the New Age has dawned.
The long-expected Messiah, born of David's line, has come.
He is Jesus of Nazareth who, after John's baptism,
    did mighty works by God's power;
    died for our sins;
    rose from the dead;
    was exalted to God's right hand;
    and will come again as judge.
Therefore let all who hear repent, and be baptized for the forgiveness of their sins.

[1] See *The Apostolic Preaching and Its Developments.*

Now, not only is this *kerygma* traceable through most of the New Testament, but our earliest Gospel, Mark, appears on examination to be simply an expansion of it. If we compare the *kerygma* of Acts 10 with the pattern of Jesus' Ministry as Mark unfolds it, the likeness is very striking. Mark begins, as the *kerygma* does, with the fulfilment of prophecy. Then, as in the *kerygma*, he opens his story of Jesus with John's baptism. The succeeding half-dozen chapters in Mark tell how 'Jesus went about doing good and healing all that were oppressed by the devil' (Acts 10.38). Next, as in Acts 10, Mark records Jesus' doings 'both in the country of the Jews and Jerusalem.' The amount of space Mark devotes to the Passion story—roughly one-third of the whole —corresponds to the stress laid on the Cross in the *kerygma*. Finally, Mark describes, as the *kerygma* did, how 'He was buried and raised on the third day' (I Cor. 15.4). If Mark's ending is lost, as most scholars believe, enough remains to show what the climax of the story was.

In short, it seems plain that Mark was following the pattern of the *kerygma*—re-telling for the benefit of his Roman readers and with the help of many stories about Jesus which he had gathered the same stupendous story of God's intervention in Jesus the Messiah which was the theme of all the apostolic preaching, Paul's message no less than Peter's (I Cor. 15.11).

II

But whence did Mark derive his stories about Jesus? At the opening of the century most scholars would have answered, 'From Peter,' and if asked for a reason, would have quoted the tradition of Papias: 'Mark, having become the interpreter of Peter, wrote down accurately everything that he remembered.' So J. A. Robinson, writing in 1902, declared:

'*Tradition points to St. Peter, the Galilean fisherman as the source of the narrative, and to St. Mark, his interpreter at Rome, as the writer of the book.*'[1]

[1] *The Study of the Gospels*, 47.

If scholars nowadays are not quite so sure of their answer, the reason lies in the one word *Formgeschichte*, or, as we call it in English, 'form criticism.' This is the new approach to the problem of Gospel origins which has helped to revivify the whole subject when source criticism (of which we shall speak presently) seemed to have done all that it could.

Form criticism is the investigation of the oral tradition which has received literary shape in our Gospels. It begins with one grand assumption—that in 'the twilight period' of oral tradition (say, A.D. 30–60) the Gospel stories and sayings circulated orally as separate units (the learned word is *pericopae*) in the various Christian communities. It concerns itself with the patterns, or forms, which these stories assumed and the causes which led to their preservation. And its aim is to take us back behind all documents to the earliest tradition about Jesus.

Let us think of it this way. When a man tells a story repeatedly, or makes a statement, he tends to develop a sort of technique. We have only to think of an old ballad, a captain's log-book, or a policeman's statement in court. So, in folk literature, our experts can classify popular stories according to their form—the way they begin, the amount of detail they employ, the way they end. Similarly, say the form critics, we may classify the stories and sayings in the Gospels, and make shrewd guesses why they were preserved.

This is the essence of form criticism which was first practised by three German scholars, Martin Dibelius, Rudolf Bultmann and K. L. Schmidt in the years just after World War I. R. H. Lightfoot and Vincent Taylor have expounded the method for English readers, and B. S. Easton and F. C. Grant have introduced American readers to it.

The form critic's first task is to *classify* the Gospel materials. Anybody can distinguish between a narrative, a parable and an aphorism; but the form critic is more systematic. Broadly speaking, he claims to detect four sorts of material in the tradition:

1. Short stories with little descriptive detail culminating in a memorable saying of Jesus. These he calls paradigms or (better)

pronouncement stories. Examples are the Question about Fasting (Mark 2), the Blessing of the Children (Mark 10) and the Tribute Money (Mark 13).

2. More detailed narratives in which a miracle of Jesus finds its setting. These he calls 'miracle stories.' Examples are the Storm on the Lake (Mark 4), Jairus's Daughter (Mark 5) and the Epileptic Boy (Mark 9).

3. Sayings of Jesus which the form critic sub-divides into wisdom-words, prophetic words, Church words, parables, etc.

4. Stories about Jesus which he calls myths or legends, i.e. narratives describing the origin of a rite or the actions of a divine being. Examples are the stories of the Baptism, the Transfiguration and the Resurrection.

Having classified his material, the form critic now essays to *recover its original form*. He assumes that the stories and sayings have suffered change and addition, as traditional material generally does, and that editors have been at work. St. Mark, for example, has supplied much of the connective tissue in his Gospel, e.g. Mark 10.46, 'And they came to Jericho.' If we are to recover the *pericopae* as they existed in the oral period, we must strip off such later supplements.

The final step is to *locate* the Gospel units in the early Christian tradition—or, as the Germans put it, to discover their *Sitz im Leben*. It is really rather naïve, the form critic assures us, to assume that biographical motives played much part in the preservation of the Gospel tradition. The earliest Christians were practical people. They needed stories about Jesus for preaching and propaganda purposes. Confronted by opponents, they required material for apologetic. And they desired Dominical guidance on many problems of Christian faith and practice. It was such needs and causes which led to the preservation and shaping of the Gospel tradition. It is in these directions we are to find the *Sitz im Leben* of the stories about Jesus, etc. Paradigms were illustrations in early Christian sermons; the sayings of Jesus were preserved as rules for Christian living; the miracle stories were models for Christian healing activities; and so on.

This is the theory of the matter; the practice of it is another question. The aim of the new Gospel science may be to discover the truth about Jesus; its effect in many quarters has been to suggest that we cannot know the truth about Him. Scepticism has vitiated it almost from the start. K. L. Schmidt began by trying to blow the Marcan framework of the Gospel story sky high,[1] and Rudolf Bultmann reached the ridiculous conclusion that we can know next to nothing about the Jesus of history.[2] Not surprisingly, therefore, in Britain, where criticism has always been more balanced, if less brilliant, than in Germany, form criticism has received a cool reception. We have been prepared to admit that the form critics' intentions were honourable, but we have been more or less agreed that their results were bad. Their sins, as we see them, are those of overdoing and ignoring.

There is truth in their theory about *pericopae*; but when they tell us in effect that all that Mark had before him was a handful of pearls which he strung on a string of his own making, they overdo it.

It may be possible to draw a broad distinction between pronouncement stories and miracle stories; but the stories about Jesus have no distinctive form, and among the sayings only the parable has a real form of its own.

It is salutary to learn that missionary preaching helped to shape the Gospel tradition; but when they rule out the biographical interest, they go much too far.

And when they find the *Sitz im Leben* of a Gospel story or saying in the life of the early Church, they hardly stop to enquire whether it had a *Sitz im Leben Jesu*—a setting in the life of Jesus —and whether it may have been preserved simply because it was true.

Of their sins of ignoring two are cardinal: one is their virtual neglect of early Church tradition, e.g. the Papias tradition about Peter; the other is their wilful disregard of the existence of eye-witnesses in the early Christian communities. Reading the form critics, we easily get the impression that when the Gospel

---

[1] *Der Rahmen der Geschichte Jesu.*   [2] *Jesus aud the Word*, 8.

tradition was taking shape, all the eye-witnesses of Jesus had either 'fallen asleep' or were in safe hiding.

The form critics make much of the creative part played by the early community in the formation of the Gospel tradition. The implication is that the Christian Church manufactured much of the Gospel material in order to explain her faith. And we cannot help asking: if early Christian faith created the Gospel record, what created Christian faith? Nor will many sensible people be persuaded by all the science of Marburg or Heidelberg that the sayings of Jesus are mere community products. 'It is not higher criticism but the higher credulity,' says T. W. Manson drily, 'that boggles at a verse in Mark and swallows without a qualm pages of pure conjecture about the primitive Christians' psychology and its workings on the pre-literary tradition.'[1]

The ordinary reader of the New Testament, then, will receive the claims and pretensions of form criticism with much reserve. He may well be grateful to the form critic for posing the right questions about the pre-literary stages of the Gospel tradition, as he may be grateful for fruitful suggestions concerning the patterns which the tradition assumed. But he must never forget that the *form* in which a story is told can never tell us whether the substance of the story is true or false. The whole method is too subjective and speculative to afford us much sure guidance. It can never in the nature of the case possess the objectivity of source criticism, to which we may now turn.

III

Form criticism is the child of the last three decades. In the first two our scholars were concerned with source criticism, with analysing out the literary sources which underlie our first three Gospels and constitute the Synoptic Problem. And in 1924—five years after form criticism began—there appeared a book containing the results—and a good deal more. B. H. Streeter's *Four Gospels* is the finest book on this subject in any language.

What had he to tell us that we did not know in 1900? At the

[1] *The Expository Times*, May, 1942.

beginning of the century what every student of divinity knows as 'the two-document theory' was at long last winning wide acceptance. Behind and beneath our Synoptic Gospels lie two documents—Mark (or an earlier form of it) and a sayings source used by Matthew and Luke and nowadays always known as Q. (Armitage Robinson's little book, *The Study of the Gospels,* published in 1902, admirably indicates the state of critical opinion then.)

Streeter's contribution was threefold: he gave an old theory its quietus; he produced a brilliant new hypothesis; and he enlarged an accepted solution so as to make it better fit the facts.

The old theory was what the Germans call *Ur-Markus*—the view that because Matthew and Luke omit certain sections of Mark and agree against him on certain minute points, they must therefore have used an earlier edition of Mark than ours. When Streeter had dealt with these omissions and agreements, most critics were convinced that the ghost of *Ur-Markus* was at last laid.

The new hypothesis was his theory of Proto-Luke.[1] Consider, said Streeter, Luke's disuse of Mark in Luke 9.51–18.14 and 6.20–8.3. Another example is 19.1–27. Consider again that Luke's Passion story owes little and his stories of the Resurrection nothing to Mark. Then, finally, remember that Q no less than Mark described John's mission, the Baptism and the Temptation, and ask yourself whether Mark is really the basis of a Gospel which began and ended without Mark and deserted him largely in the middle. Are not the non-Marcan bits of Luke—what we call Q and L (special Luke)—the real backbone of the Third Gospel?

So Streeter reasoned: then came his theory. There were two stages in the making of the Third Gospel: (*a*) a first draft composed of Q and L—'Proto-Luke'—and (*b*) the completed Gospel.

---

[1] An important precursor of Streeter was Professor A. M. Perry of Bangor, Maine, who in *The Sources of Luke's Passion Narrative* (1920) ably argued that the Third Evangelist had at his disposal an independent Passion narrative. This is one of the corner-stones of the Proto-Luke theory.

About A.D. 60 (ran Streeter's guess) St. Luke, who had picked up valuable tradition about Jesus in Caesarea (during Paul's detention there) combined this L material with the sayings-source Q to form an embryonic Gospel. Five or ten years later, coming on Mark, he fitted extracts from it into this QL framework, adding the Preface and the Birth stories. The final result was our Third Gospel.

Could the hypothesis be established? Many things in the Gospel consisted well with it (as Vincent Taylor showed in *Behind the Third Gospel*): the alternation of Marcan and non-Marcan strips; Luke's preference for Q or L versions of incidents also in Mark (e.g. the Rejection at Nazareth); the six-fold date in Luke 3.1f. (which reads like the beginning of a book); the curious position of the genealogy (to be expected among the Birth stories); Luke's omission of some 250 verses from Mark; the fact that Proto-Luke when printed out seems to present a fairly continuous story, etc.

But, as the scholars proceeded to examine the hypothesis, other facts made them give pause. The first section of the so-called Proto-Luke (3.1–4.30) is not solidly non-Marcan, as we might expect if the theory is correct; and indeed the whole Galilean section (3.1–9.50) owes much more to Mark than appears at first sight. The 'central section' (9.51–18.14) is not so close-knit a narrative as had been claimed. And even in the Passion story (22.14–24.10) where Luke deviates twelve times from Mark's order and uses only 27 per cent. of his words, it is by no means clear that Mark is not Luke's basic source. There are echoes of Mark at all the high points of the narrative.

So, twenty-five years after its propounding, the hypothesis remains hypothetical. If scholars like T. W. Manson and C. J. Cadoux have accepted it, J. M. Creed and W. Bussmann have rejected it. It has not been disproved, but certain pillars on which it rested have weakened under criticism; and few scholars are prepared in constructive work to commit themselves to its truth. Yet the hypothesis is not only interesting, but important. For, if it were established, we should have in Proto-Luke an authority for the Life of Jesus as old as Mark, independent of it, and of comparable value. We may hope that in the next decade or two we may have a decision on it one way or the other from scholars ready to undertake the linguistic spade-work which such a decision will involve.

Streeter's third great contribution was the four-document hypothesis.[1]

The two-document theory is sound, so far as it goes. But does it go far enough? Subtract Marcan and Q matter from our First and Third Gospels, and we are left with Matthew's special tradition and Luke's special tradition, which we may call M and L. L, as we have seen, may well be the tradition of Caesarea as gleaned by Luke. But what about M?

Streeter was dissatisfied by the current assumption that there were only two sources behind the Synoptic Gospels—'the Big Two,' Mark and Q. Mark emanated from Rome, Q very possibly from Antioch. But is it not likely that the two great Palestinian churches of Jerusalem and Caesarea had also traditions of their own which found a place in our Gospels? Would it not be more scientific to speak of four sources instead of two?

Clearly L was a distinct source, whether written (Streeter) or oral (V. Taylor and T. W. Manson). Is it not probable that Matthew had a special sayings collection too? Consider Matthew's version of, say, the Beatitudes, the Lord's Prayer, and the parable of the Lost Sheep. They are like yet also unlike their counterparts in Luke. Does not the very existence of such parallel versions in Matthew point to his use of another collection of Jesus' sayings besides Q? This was Streeter's starting point. His conclusion was that not only did 'Matthew' use a sayings collection, to be called M, but that it emanated from Jerusalem and was to be dated about A.D. 65.

[1] The well-known American scholar, Professor E. De Witt Burton of Chicago, had, as early as 1904, propounded a four-document theory of the Synoptic Gospels. Differing from Streeter's, it posited these four sources. (a) Mark; (b) M, a special Matthaean source; (c) P, a Peraean source, found mostly in Luke's central section (9.51–18.14); and (d) G, a Galilean document, found in Luke 3–8. But Burton's source analysis never won wide recognition.

The case for M is as follows.[1] We start from passages (like those already mentioned) where Q seems to have been used yet where word-for-word agreement between Matthew and Luke is small; and the argument is threefold:

First, these passages are best explained, if instead of trying to attribute everything to Q (or editorial modifications of it) we assume two sayings collections, Q and M, which partly overlapped.

Second, this assumption is strengthened by our knowledge of Matthew's literary methods. We know that he often 'conflated' (interwove) Mark and Q. So we may reasonably suppose that in the passages in question he was conflating Q with some other source.

Third, in passages where we suspect the use of this other source, we find a decidedly Judaistic tinge (see, for example, Matt. 5.17–20 and 10.6).

A good case can therefore be made out for Matthew's use of a special sayings source. To it we may assign three-fifths of the Sermon on the Mount, much of the Mission Charge in Matt. 10, most of the indictment of the Scribes and Pharisees in 23, and sundry other sayings. (The *narrative* additions peculiar to Matthew Streeter assigns not to M but to the local church tradition in Antioch where the first Gospel was probably written.)

The logical conclusion of all this was a four-source solution of the Synoptic Problem to replace the two-source theory. Streeter went farther—he spoke of a four-*document* theory: Mark to be connected with Rome, Q with Antioch, M with Jerusalem and L with Caesarea.

Such a theory (Streeter claimed) would do three things: it would fit all the facts better than the two-document theory; by connecting our Gospels with four great centres of early Christianity, it would explain how they inevitably found their way into the Canon; and it would materially broaden the basis for the life

[1] On the M Hypothesis see F. C. Grant's brilliant article in *The Expository Times,* July, 1935; also his own book *The Growth of the Gospels* (1933).

and teaching of Christ, since we could not now afford to ignore the tradition not found in the 'Big Two.'

How has the theory fared at the hands of the critics? If not a few scholars had hesitations about the Proto-Luke hypothesis, most are agreed that the four-document theory is true in substance. Their one doubt is about the use of the word 'document.' Mark was a document, Q almost certainly so; but we cannot prove that L and M were written sources. They may have been simply cycles of oral tradition. But Streeter's main contention— that four distinct sources underlie our Synoptic Gospels—has not been seriously contested. Henceforth the Big Two must give place to the Big Four; and when we discuss our Lord's teaching, we must ask not merely, What do Mark and Q say? but, What do Mark and Q and M and L report? This is indubitable and great gain.

Note: During the years 1925–31 Wilhelm Bussmann of Germany wrote three books on the Synoptic sources in which he propounded a very elaborate theory of sources. Not only did he trace three stages in the literary evolution of Mark:

G: a short basis used by Luke,
B: a Galilean revision of G, used by Matthew, and
E: our canonical Mark, as finally revised in Rome,

but he split up Q into two sources: T (a Greek source used by Matthew and Luke) and R (an Aramaic source—perhaps Papias's *Logia*—used in two different Greek translations by Matthew and Luke). Luke had also a special source, S, and Matthew a special source M. This very complicated theory has not commended itself to the British scholars who have examined it. (See Vincent Taylor's two reviews of it in the *Hibbert Journal* for July, 1931, and January, 1932; T. W. Manson in *The Sayings of Jesus*, 20f., and W. Manson, *Jesus the Messiah*, 22f.).

We may round off this section of our chapter with a brief summary of present views about the date, provenance and authorship of the Gospels. As our four sources are to be dated roughly as follows: Mark, 65–70, Q, *c.* 50, M, *c.* 65, and L, *c.* 60, so the completed Gospels are usually dated thus:

Mark: 65–70
Luke: *c.* 80
Matthew: *c.* 85.

As to place of writing, all agree that Mark was written in Rome; there is much to be said for the view that Matthew was written in Antioch;[1] and tradition says that Luke wrote his Gospel in Achaea.[2]

The First Gospel is anonymous, though the name of Matthew was possibly connected with it because Matthew 'composed the Logia' (Q?) which was one of its main sources. The Second Gospel was the work of John Mark, the Jerusalemite friend of both Paul and Peter. And though this, as we shall see later, has been widely denied in Germany, the Third Gospel, with its sequel Acts is to be attributed to Luke, the beloved physician.

IV

By way of epilogue to this chapter we may treat, very briefly, an issue much discussed in the last fifty years: that of the Gospels and history.

At the beginning of the century, while the spirit of nineteenth-century Liberalism still dominated our Gospel scholarship, the aim of the critics was to get back behind the Gospel stories to the 'bare facts' about Jesus—the facts minus the theological theory that the New Testament writers may have imposed on them. Denney might warn them that they were pursuing a will-o'-the-wisp:

'A fact of which there is absolutely no theory is a fact which stands out of relation to everything in the universe, a fact which has no connection with any part of our experience; it is a blank

[1] Streeter, *The Four Gospels*, 500ff.

[2] Streeter (*op. cit.*, 534) suggests Corinth, and guesses that 'his excellency' Theophilus was Governor of Achaea, and resided in Corinth.

unintelligibility, a rock in the sky, a mere irrelevance in the mind of man.'[1]

But they were not to be put off. Historical science (they believed), could, by stripping off later theological accretions and legends, get back to a neutral and undogmatic version of Jesus. The assumption was that there was a real and great difference between the Jesus of history and the Christ of faith.

This was the spirit of what the Germans call *Historismus*, and it is now *démodé*. We now realise that the liberal attempt to drive a wedge between Jesus and Christianity by producing a neutral account of Jesus derived from a careful sifting of the Gospels is foredoomed to failure. All proper historical writing is a record of *interpreted* facts: history written without presuppositions of one kind or another is a chimaera. This is pre-eminently true of the Gospel history. The form critics have reminded us that in the Gospels record and revelation cannot be separated. The writers aim to tell us about Jesus of Nazareth, a first-century Jew; but they are no less clear that this Jew was none other than the Messiah and divine Son of God. The facts about Him which they record are facts plus faith; and all our Gospels, Mark no less than John, were written 'from faith to faith.'

But if in the Gospels we have not 'bare facts,' but 'facts plus faith,' i.e. interpreted history, then the one great question is: Have the Evangelists interpreted the facts rightly or wrongly? Is it not possible (the sceptic may say) that the facts about Jesus have been so transformed by the alchemy of Christian faith as to be irrecoverably lost?

To this question we may reply that it is on all counts more probable that the faith arose out of the facts than that the faith created them. But we may go farther. We may point, first of all, to the whole atmosphere and setting of the Gospel Story. So far as we can judge, it is primitive and Palestinian: it reflects the religious and social conditions of first-century Palestine. This is some guarantee of its reliability. A second weighty consideration in its favour is that the Gospel record (and indeed the whole New

[1] *Studies in Theology*, 106.

Testament) is built upon the apostolic *kerygma*, i.e. a summary of tradition about Jesus which, in such passages as I Cor. 15.3ff., we can trace back to within a few years of the Crucifixion. And a third point which tells strongly in favour of the historical worth of the Gospel picture of Jesus is to be derived from the Evangelists' use of the argument from Old Testament prophecy. All the Evangelists claim that in Jesus the Old Testament finds its fulfilment. Yet (as Rawlinson says) precisely because their telling of the story is controlled by the authentic memory of the original facts about Jesus, they do not dare to represent the Old Testament prophecies as having been literally, or conventionally, fulfilled in Jesus. The Messiah (to take only one example) was to be a King:

> *They all were looking for a King*
> *To slay their foes and lift them high—*

The Evangelists do affirm that He was a King, but they no less affirm that His Kingship was 'not of this world,' and that His royalty was to be construed in terms of service. We may conclude that the Christ of the earliest Christian tradition was no dream figure conjured up from Old Testament prophecy.

All these considerations point in one direction. The Gospel record is rooted in history. 'Record and Revelation, history and interpretation, cannot in the Gospels be separated; but the control of history is everywhere present. The Cross, which lies at the heart of the story, is beyond question a stark and dreadful reality. Who could have been found to invent such a paradox as that of a crucified Messiah? The earliest witnesses to Jesus of Nazareth were no followers of "cunningly devised fables." They were men who were set to bear witness to the truth.'[1]

---

[1] Rawlinson, *Christ in the Gospels*, 118f. On the whole subject, see C. H. Dodd, *History and the Gospel*.

V

The Life of Christ in the Twentieth Century

✳

'SIR,' said the Greeks to Philip, 'we would see Jesus.' It is a
request that echoes down the centuries. No life has ever fascinated
men like that of Jesus, none has produced more books. Who
shall number the 'lives' of Christ that appeared in the nineteenth
century? And still, in this twentieth century, now half run, the
century of the two greatest wars in history when more and more
men seem preoccupied with science and the production of lethal
weapons, the fascination of the story of Jesus continues, and men,
learned and unlearned, study anew those frail and fragmentary
records of Jesus and His words which we call the Four Gospels,
in hope of learning more or of surprising some secret not yet
disclosed to previous students of the records.

It is the purpose of this chapter to pick out the ten most
important contributions to the story of Jesus in the twentieth
century. Not all of them are 'lives' in the strict sense. Inevitably
we shall omit some that others will consider better worthy of
inclusion; but all of them add something to our knowledge or
see Jesus from an angle that is new. And anyone who likes can
add to our selected ten.

The ten we choose, in chronological order, are:

William Sanday, *Outlines of the Life of Christ* (1905).
James Denney, *Jesus and the Gospel* (1908).
Albert Schweitzer, *The Quest of the Historical Jesus* (1910).
T. R. Glover, *The Jesus of History* (1917).
Joseph Klausner, *Jesus of Nazareth* (1925).
Rudolf Bultmann, *Jesus* (1925); Eng. Tr., *Jesus and the Word*
(1934).

Middleton Murry, *Life of Jesus* (1926).

T. W. Manson, *The Teaching of Jesus* (1931).

Maurice Goguel, *The Life of Jesus* (1933; French, 1932).

Rudolf Otto, *The Kingdom of God and the Son of Man* (1934; Eng. Tr., 1938).

I

Our first book is, of course, a reprint of the famous article which Dr. William Sanday of Oxford contributed to the second volume of Hastings' *Dictionary of the Bible* in 1899. In some ways, it is the classical treatment of our theme in English. The 'layout' of the material could hardly be bettered, and the tone of the whole is eminently wise. What sort of man is needed to write the life of Christ? Sanday answered: 'A Newman with science and adequate knowledge.' No man of his time came nearer that ideal than Sanday himself. Wide learning, exact scholarship, a luminous style—all were his. He had, moreover, that rarer quality in a critic—sagacity and judgment. This 'life' is, in his own phrase, 'liberal-conservative.' No attempt is made to force the person and work of Jesus into the Procrustes bed of a particular theory. The teaching, the miracles, the Virgin Birth and the Resurrection are all discussed with profound sense. Sanday wrote before Schweitzer had called attention to the eschatology of the Gospels, and I fancy that if he had ever fulfilled his ambition to expand this 'outline' into a full-scale life of Christ, he would have written otherwise on various issues, the kingdom of God among them; but, as an example of reverent New Testament scholarship at the beginning of the century there is none better.

II

Books which strike a blow for orthodoxy seldom create such a furore as those less obviously 'on the side of the angels.' Our next book, Denney's *Jesus and the Gospel*, is a case in point. Denney was probably the greatest New Testament scholar Scotland has produced, and his book was a strong and timely antidote to the 'new theologies' then in the air. It is not a 'life,' but it is centrally concerned with Christ in the Gospels. 'The idea I have,' he wrote, 'is to show that the Gospel as the Apostles preached and believed it can be verified in the mind of Jesus.' No writer in English ever performed that task more triumphantly. The core of the book is a careful study of the mind of Christ as revealed in the two primary Gospel sources, Mark and Q. One by one the relevant sayings of Jesus from the Baptism to the Passion are reviewed until, at the end, Denney can claim that cumulatively they disclose a Person 'who is not only equal to the place which Christian faith assigns Him but who assumes that place naturally and spontaneously as His own.' After forty years that argument remains as clear and strong and convincing as ever.

III

Two years afterwards there appeared in English a book by a young theologian from Alsace named Albert Schweitzer (the German edition was published in 1906). *The Quest of the Historical Jesus* at once created a sensation. Three-quarters of it were devoted to a survey of the life-of-Jesus research (in German and French). It was the last quarter which expounded Schweitzer's own views—and made the stir.

And no wonder. The real Jesus (said Schweitzer) was a strange, imperious figure obsessed by an apocalyptic dream in which the 'birth pangs' of the New Age, the Parousia, the Last Judgment and the supernatural kingdom of God followed each other in swift succession. He died to make that dream come true. Though from the Baptism on He knew He would be the Messiah, He kept it secret. When He sent out the Twelve, He expected the end of the world would come before they had been round the cities of Israel (Matt. 10.23). When it did not happen, He altered His forecast. Convinced now that He must endure the pangs Himself and die if the end were to come, He marched on Jerusalem not of His own freewill, but of dogmatic necessity. The secret of Messiahship, disclosed to the Twelve at Caesarea Philippi, was betrayed by Judas to the priests, and Jesus flung Himself on the Cross, hoping that His death would force God to bring all to pass. *Deo aliter visum.* He died in dereliction. That is His victory. But what of His ethical teaching? That, replies Schweitzer, was only 'an ethic of the interval'—till the supernatural kingdom came. The kingdom itself needs no ethics.

It is a shattering picture. But is it true? Four grave charges can be levelled against it. (1) Schweitzer uses his sources uncritically. His exegesis practically begins and ends with Matthew, particularly Matt. 10.23, a saying of very dubious value. (2) He turns a Nelson eye on all evidence in the Synoptics which proclaims the kingdom a present reality in the ministry of Jesus. (3) He makes nonsense of the ethic of Jesus. And (4) he makes Jesus the deluded victim of a fixed eschatological programme.

If Schweitzer says that the liberal Jesus never existed, we may retort that his eschatological Jesus never did either. Yet Schweitzer did one really important thing: he compelled scholars to face the problem of eschatology in the Gospels, and challenged them to produce a better interpretation than his own. Every writer since 1910 has had to meet that challenge.

IV

Glover's *Jesus of History* may seem too slight and unsystematic a book to be ranked among our chosen ten. Yet what book in its day had a wider influence, and what book more vividly fulfilled the promise of its title? 'He let me see Jesus,' said Denney of his old teacher, A. B. Bruce. Glover did precisely this for many of his contemporaries. Jesus the man, in all His grace, simplicity, sympathy and charm; a Jesus fond of little children, loving common men and common things; a Teacher of genius who saw and thought in pictures; a Jesus who discovered God the Father, rested wholly on Him, and died to reveal Him—this was the portrait Glover painted. A liberal portrait? Yes; but what a spring-like freshness there was in it! More than any other, Glover humanised Jesus, and made Him infinitely attractive and alive.

But—and it is a serious but—Glover let us see only one side of Jesus and the Gospel. That he saw Jesus through Greek rather than Jewish eyes is true but understandable. What we do find it harder to understand is his blindness to the theology of the Gospels. Glover has no real idea what the Kingdom of God means in the Gospels; and so far as eschatology is concerned, Schweitzer might never have written. Glover does not see that the person of Jesus is integral to the Gospel. The Jesus of history is an incomparably bigger figure than Glover's charming canvas shows.

V

'Jesus was not a Christian,' observed Wellhausen; 'He was a Jew.' The next writer, Joseph Klausner, himself a Jew, never lets us forget this.[1] Try as he may to be fair, his *Jesus of Nazareth* is really propaganda for Judaism. The Christian reader knows what to expect, and need be neither surprised nor shocked when Klausner claims that all Jesus' ethical teaching can be paralleled somewhere or other in Jewish sources, and dismisses the Virgin Birth, the miracles and the tradition of the empty tomb as legends. For Klausner, Jesus is an unorthodox Galilean 'Rab' who, mistakenly believing Himself the Messiah, went up to Jerusalem, expecting to triumph, but was seized by the Sadducean priests and crucified by the Romans. The greatness of Jesus, he says, lies in His ethic. 'If ever the day should come that this ethical code be stripped of its wrappings of miracle and mysticism, the book of the ethics of Jesus will be one of the choicest treasures in the literature of Israel for all time.'

The value of this book lies not in these *ex parte* judgments, but in the masterly delineation of the background—political, economic and religious—of the Gospel story. His translator, Dr. Danby, rightly claims that 'it represents the best that unimpeachable Jewish learning has to show.' It is a liberal education in rabbinics.

[1] Much has been done in this half-century to illumine our Lord's teaching from Jewish literature. Here pride of place must go to Strack and Billerbeck's great *Kommentar zum N.T. aus Talmud and Midrasch* (1922), which provides abundant illustrative materials from the teaching of the Jewish rabbis. The English reader will learn much along these lines from C. G. Montefiore's *The Synoptic Gospels* (2nd Ed., 1927) and from the same writer's *Rabbinic Literature and Gospel Teachings* (1930). I. Abrahams' two volumes called *Studies in Pharisaism and the Gospels* (1917 and 1924) are also valuable.

VI

In 1926 came the German Bultmann's *Jesus*. When we learn that Bultmann, the most sceptical critic since Strauss, is also one of the 'dialectical' theologians, we are tempted to murmur, 'Is Saul also among the prophets?' For, in Bultmann's view, there is not much in the Gospels we can trust. Most of it is to be ascribed to the creation of the early Christian communities.

In spite of this, Bultmann feels he is in a position to reconstruct the message of Jesus. It is an eschatological gospel. Such ideas as the infinite worth of personality or the development of man towards an ideal are foreign to it. Its theme is the coming of the supernatural Kingdom of God (God's gift, not man's achievement) and of the summons to man for decision in view of the impending crisis. Obedience (*Gehorsam*) to God's demands—that is the essence of Jesus' ethic. But who is this Person who summons to decision? He is the prophet Jesus, the Bearer of the decisive Word of God to men, which sets men in the eschatological Now and challenges them to decide for or against God.

We have said that Bultmann's whole approach is vitiated by excessive scepticism. The charge which Windisch and others have brought against him is that he confuses critical scholarship with theological exegesis. The charge has point. Years ago Loisy complained that Harnack's Jesus was but the reflection of a liberal Protestant face. Bultmann's Jesus might be said to be the reflection of a Barthian face. *C'est dialectique, mais ce n'est pas histoire.*

VII

When you put down Bultmann and take up the next book, Middleton Murry's *Life of Jesus*, you pass from the New Testament Seminar in Marburg to Fleet Street at its best. In place of the imperious Prophet calling to *Entscheidung*, there stands a high-souled Man of Genius who, knowing God as His Father, would have all men share His secret. Gone too, is the historical scepticism; for though Murry rejects St. John's evidence, he rightly discerns the essential honesty of Mark's story.

Murry is a sort of post-Schweitzerian Renan. Thus, we are reminded of Renan and Schweitzer, when half-way through Murry's *Life*, Jesus the Teacher, disappointed by the non-appearance of the Son of Man and the people's rejection of His gospel of God's Fatherhood, assumes the role of an apocalyptic *Messias futurus*, who must die like God's Servant if the present world order is to end and the transcendent kingdom appear. And when he tells us that the betrayal was 'a put-up job' between Judas and the priests, or describes the immeasurably great Man dying in dereliction, we think of the brilliant Alsatian.

Murry's book is a picture of how Jesus appears to a fine-minded and accomplished man of letters. One reads it for its descriptive messages of quite astonishing beauty. It is written with a manifest admiration for Jesus 'divinest when He most is man.' 'We shall look like men,' says Murry, 'on the man Jesus. He will stand our scrutiny. Keep our heads as high as we can, they shall be bowed at the last.'

VIII

The next book, T. W. Manson's *The Teaching of Jesus* (1931), written in a Northumberland manse, is perhaps the most original book in our ten. Manson broke new ground in several ways. To begin with, he took seriously Streeter's four-document theory and studied our Lord's sayings according to the four sources, Mark, Q, M and L. Then he proceeded to classify them according to their addressees (the general public, His opponents, His disciples), with at least one challenging result. Liberalism had often assumed that the burden of Jesus' preaching to the multitudes was, 'God is your Father and you are all brothers.' Manson's studies led him to very different conclusions. The Fatherhood of God was not a doctrine Jesus preached to the general public; it was a mystery disclosed in private to the disciples. 'For them, He made the Father real, not by argument or by much speaking, but because it was obvious that the Father was the supreme reality of His own life.' Manson's other startling thesis was that the title Son of Man in the Gospels is a *collective* title, a continuation indeed of the Old Testament doctrine of the 'saved and saving Remnant.' Derived from Dan. 7 and used by Jesus only after Caesarea Philippi, it denoted Jesus and His disciples as the new Israel. But His followers failed to rise to the height of their Leader's demands, and at last, at the Cross, Jesus stood alone as the true incarnation of the Son of Man. He was rejected and crucified. But His death proved the birth pangs of the Son of Man, and after the Resurrection the Son of Man found new and glorious embodiment in the Church, His own Body, of which He is the Head.

So stated, Manson's theory may not win wide acceptance, but his emphasis on the *societary* side of the title contains deep truth, and must command the respectful attention of all New Testament scholars.

IX

From England we turn now to France. In 1932, after the form critics had been telling us for a decade that we could not write a life of Christ, the French scholar M. Goguel produced one of nearly six hundred pages. His *Vie de Jésus* has been acclaimed as the best of its kind between the wars. On the score of mere scholarship this may be so; but the 'life' is at once lopsided and disappointing. Lopsided because one half of his space goes on prolegomena; and disappointing because it relies so much on guess-work and speculative psychology and ends up with a Jesus not markedly different from Schweitzer's.

Goguel's Jesus began His Galilean ministry as an eschatological prophet who proclaimed an imminent Kingdom of God and expected a speedy fulfilment of Matt. 10.23. After a time of initial popularity, Herod's menaces drove Him to flight, and when He refused to play the role of Messianic King following the Galilean Lord's Supper, the people forsook Him. But after Peter's confession the Prophet turned into One who believed that He was destined, after suffering, to appear as the Son of Man and inaugurate the supernatural Kingdom of God. After a visit to

Jerusalem at the Feast of Tabernacles and a retreat to Perea, He made His final appeal to Jerusalem on the ensuing Passover (A.D. 28). It failed. His enemies had Him arrested and crucified, and He died believing God had deserted Him.

We may be forgiven if as Christians we refuse to follow M. Goguel in his conjectures. Yet his 'life' has fine sentences, as witness this one: 'Jesus did not believe that He was the Messiah *although* He had to suffer; He believed that He was the Messiah *because* He had to suffer. This is the great paradox, the great originality, of His Gospel.'

X

The last book in our list, Otto's *The Kingdom of God and the Son of Man*, has been hailed as a turning-point in the study of the Gospels. Certainly it is a very important contribution, and it is therefore unfortunate that, for many of us, it should suffer from two grave faults: (*a*) Otto's adoption of a dubious Synoptic theory (Bussmann's) and (*b*) his conviction that the key to the Story of Jesus is to be found in the Book of Enoch—a view which Bultmann for several good reasons dismisses as 'fantastic.'

On three issues—eschatology, the Messiahship, and the Last Supper—Otto has true and notable things to say. With Schweitzer he maintains that the Kingdom of God is an eschatological idea; but he sees, as Schweitzer did not, that the Kingdom is already present and active in the ministry of Jesus. He thus anticipates C. H. Dodd in the doctrine of 'realized eschatology' which has so vivified and illumined our study of the Gospels. Second, in portraying Jesus as 'the eschatological redeemer,' he finds (as of course Goguel and many others before had found) the key to our Lord's conception of His person in a profound synthesis of the Son of Man with the Servant of the Lord. And, third, he interprets the Last Supper as an act of 'prophetic symbolism' in which Jesus not only predicts His atoning death but, by inviting His disciples to eat and drink, offers them 'a share in the power of the broken Christ.' Along these three lines and in many smaller points of exegesis (e.g. the hard saying preserved in

Matt. 11.12; Luke 17.21) Otto has set New Testament scholars thinking in most fruitful ways, and his last book may well prove to be as important as his *Idea of the Holy*.

XI

Having completed our survey, we are painfully conscious of omissions, of important studies on various aspects of the Gospels which have not figured among our chosen ten: Benjamin Bacon's lucid *Story of Jesus* (1927), with its bias against eschatology and its attempt to make our Lord's message purely ethical and religious; Shirley J. Case's new 'biography' of *Jesus* (1927), with its protest against 'documentarianism' and its emphasis on 'social environment' as the key to the life of Jesus; C. H. Dodd's *Parables of the Kingdom* (1935), setting the parables of Jesus in a framework of 'realised eschatology'; Vincent Taylor's *Jesus and His Sacrifice* (1939), expounding the Passion sayings of Jesus for this generation as Denney had done for the preceding one; George Ogg's scholarly *Chronology of the Public Ministry of Jesus* (1940), perhaps the best study of this subject since C. H. Turner's classical article in *Hastings' Dictionary*; William Manson's difficult but rewarding *Jesus the Messiah* (1943); John Knox's two admirable studies, *The Man Christ Jesus* (1941) and *Christ the Lord* (1945); John Wick Bowman's *Intention of Jesus* (1943), fit sequel to T. W. Manson's book, showing conclusively that the high purpose of Jesus was to found the Church; and so on. But looking back over our ten, we are struck by one highly significant fact. The last quarter of the century has produced only one big critical life of Jesus—Goguel's. One might have imagined that the writing of a life would be the crowning ambition of every *Neutestamentler* worthy of his salt. Why then are the experts in our day apparently so reluctant to make the great venture?

It is not enough to answer that they realise that the materials at their disposal are not sufficient for a full-dress biography. This is true; but it was true also in the nineteenth century, when innumerable 'lives' appeared. Part of the answer is undoubtedly to be found in the single word, *Formgeschichte*. Before its advent

58

after World War I, the task seemed easier. So long as scholars believed that in Mark, the earliest Gospel, they had a firm and reliable outline of Christ's Ministry, they had a foundation on which to build. But the form critics—and especially K. L. Schmidt in his *Der Rahmen der Geschichte Jesu* (1919)—made scholars much less sure of their belief. There arose an uneasy suspicion that Schmidt and others had 'knocked the Marcan scaffolding to pieces' and left us with only a handful of scattered *pericopae* before the Passion story was reached.

Now it is true that the Marcan hypothesis has taken some hard knocks; but Schmidt's view is a great exaggeration. As C. H. Dodd showed (in *The Expository Times*, XLIII, June, 1932), 'the Marcan order does represent a genuine succession of events, within which movement and development can be traced.' Mark still can be a basis on which to build.

No, form criticism is not a complete answer. Perhaps the influence of Barthianism must also be reckoned with. For Barth actually suggests that 'so far as we can get back to the historical Jesus, there is nothing remarkable to be found in His Life and character and teaching' (D. M. Baillie, *God was in Christ*, 36). Form criticism, Barthianism—perhaps the real reason lies, as Vincent Taylor suggests, elsewhere, in a sort of intellectual sloth, a lack of courage to 're-tell the Story of Stories to a dying world.'

Whatever the reasons, the present reluctance to make the attempt seems very regrettable. In many ways we are in a better position to do so than we were a century ago. The textual critics have provided us with a reliable text. The source critics, and particularly Streeter, have analysed our Synoptic Gospels into their component parts, and helped us to appraise the underlying sources. We know a great deal more about Pharisees and Sadducees and the background of the Gospel story generally. Thanks to Schweitzer, Otto and Dodd, we have a much better understanding of the eschatological data in the Gospels and of key concepts like the Kingdom of God and the Son of Man. We understand the parables better and their *Sitz im Leben Jesu*. And so far as the miracles are concerned, we have moved far (witness the books of D. S. Cairns and C. S. Lewis) from the position of Matthew Arnold and others in the nineteenth century.

These items are all on the credit side. Of course, on the debit side, many difficulties remain. We are not yet sure how far we can use the Fourth Gospel as a historical source, though we are much less contemptuous of it than some critics were fifty years ago. There is the problem of the Virgin Birth. Shall that particular tradition find a place in a critical Life, or must we relegate it to an appendix? Above all, granting that Mark can be trusted to afford a broadly trustworthy outline of the Ministry, how are we to fit into it the narratives, sayings and parables from our other sources?

Yet, when all difficulties are admitted, the task should not be so daunting as it seems. To be sure, we cannot make a closely articulated, chronological scheme of the Ministry, with precise dates accurately inserted. But there is much we can do. We can, with some accuracy, reconstruct the background of the Early Years. We can depict the general trend of the Ministry. We can give some account of the main themes in our Lord's teaching. We can pick out the main crises, like Caesarea Philippi, in the Life, and of course we have material to describe the last and greatest crisis which we call the Passion and Resurrection.

The present writer has recently made a very modest attempt to do all this.[1] He is very conscious how inadequate it is. But his hope is that others much abler than himself will arise to better his performance. There is nothing our world needs more than a fresh and truer vision of the Life of lives.

[1] *The Work and Words of Jesus* (1950).

VI

St. Paul in the Twentieth Century

*

S O M E eighty-five years ago Renan delivered himself of this
judgment:

'After having been, owing to Protestantism, for three hundred
years the supreme Christian doctor, Paul sees in our days his reign
coming to an end. The writings of Paul have been a peril and a
stumbling-block, the cause of the principal defects of Christian
theology; Paul is the father of the subtle Augustine, the arid
Aquinas, the sombre Calvinist, the sour Jansenist, and the
ferocious theology which predestinates to damnation.'

It is obvious that Renan did not love 'the ugly little Jew' from
Tarsus. But it is no less obvious that the father of such a formidable progeny must himself have been a very considerable man,
not to be easily prophesied out of his greatness by an accomplished writer who, as one of his critics observed, 'cared more
for beauty than for truth.' In fact, of course, the prophecy has
not been fulfilled. From Renan's day to ours no year has passed
without adding fresh volumes to the already immense library
about St. Paul. Renan underrated the true magnitude of his man,
and it may safely be predicted that, so long as Christianity lasts,
men will turn afresh to these letters written from Corinth,
Ephesus and Rome which even his enemies had to admit were
'weighty and powerful' (II Cor. 10.10). Karl Barth saw deeper
into Paul's secret when he wrote in the Preface to his now
famous commentary on the Romans:[1]

'Paul, as a child of his age, addressed his contemporaries. As
prophet and apostle of the Kingdom of God, he veritably speaks

---

[1] *The Epistle to the Romans*, I.

61

to all men of every age. . . . If we rightly understand ourselves, our problems are the problems of Paul; and if we be enlightened by the brightness of his answers, those answers must be ours.'

What was he, this peripatetic little tent-maker from Tarsus, whose writings have been such a ferment in Christian theology for nineteen hundred years? Mystic or mystery-monger, ecstatic or eschatologist, systematic theologian elaborating dogmas or hero of piety, truest interpreter of the Gospel or its greatest perverter? All these views have had their champions in the last fifty years; and we shall have to consider them. But we must first turn to the letters themselves and see what light fifty years have shed on problems of authenticity and provenance.

I

Turn up a New Testament Introduction of fifty years ago and you will probably find that the first words on any of St. Paul's letters deal with authenticity. Open one of recent vintage, and in only one or two cases does the question seem to need serious discussion. The change is significant. In 1900, despite the magnificent commentaries of Lightfoot, the ghost of Baur of Tübingen (who acknowledged as genuine only Romans, Galatians and I and II Corinthians) was not yet finally laid, and there were still cranks like the Dutchman Van Manen capable of denying the genuineness of the whole Pauline Corpus.[1]

Nowadays even critics like Dibelius with no bias to conservatism in Biblical studies are willing to admit II Thessalonians as genuine, and the only letters over which real doubt hangs are Ephesians and the Pastorals.

It must be confessed that the controversy about Ephesians has not made much headway. In the last fifty years most British scholars (Moffatt was a notable exception) have found the arguments against its authenticity indecisive. In Germany, and in some American circles, many ascribe the letter to a Paulinist. And some like Dean Inge confess that when they read the letter in English

[1] In the columns of *The Encyclopædia Biblica*.

they are sure it is Paul's, but when they read it in Greek their doubts awake.

One of the big difficulties, if we deny the letter to St. Paul, is that we must postulate the existence of an unknown writer who was at once a fairly slavish copier of Paul's letter to the Colossians and a man of such original mind that he could produce what Coleridge called 'one of the divinest compositions of man.' In his *Meaning of Ephesians* (1933), E. J. Goodspeed produced a theory to meet some of these difficulties. After Paul's death, he says, the man and his letters were practically forgotten. Then, about A.D. 85, the appearance of the Acts of the Apostles revived interest in him. This opportunity a Christian in Asia Minor (Goodspeed thinks he may even have been Onesimus, the runaway slave) embraced with alacrity. A lover of Paul, he already had Colossians almost by rote, and he now decided to search the other churches for further letters of the Apostle. The letters which he thus rescued from oblivion convinced him that this spiritual treasure must be made available to a wider circle, with an introduction gathering up the quintessence of Paul's thought. This introduction, inevitably reminiscent of Colossians, was the Epistle to the Ephesians.

This theory might explain (1) the similarity of Ephesians to Colossians and (2) the difference in style; but it contains too many 'perhapses' to be altogether convincing. (Can we believe that Paul was so soon and completely forgotten?) The ordinary reader must ask himself whether it is more convincing than that which the Church accepted unhesitatingly for eighteen hundred years.[1]

We turn now to the problem of the Pastorals. Was Paul the Pastor?

Since 1900 the scholars have divided themselves into three camps:

(*a*) Those who (like the Anglican Parry and the Roman Catholics Meinertz and Spicq) accept the full Pauline authorship.

---

[1] Klausner can find no good reason for denying the authenticity of Ephesians; *From Jesus to Paul*, 242ff.

(*b*) Those who (like Dibelius and many German scholars) regard the letters as pseudonymous and date them in the first half of the second century.

(*c*) Those who (like Harrison, Falconer and E. F. Scott) regard the letters as amplifications by a Paulinist of genuine fragments of St. Paul.

The case against their authenticity is fourfold: (1) historical: we cannot fit the letters into the historical framework supplied by Acts; (2) ecclesiastical: the church organisation in the Pastorals seems too late for Paul's time; (3) doctrinal: Paul, it has been said, is inspired, the Pastor simply orthodox; (4) linguistic: the Pastor's style and especially his vocabulary differ greatly from Paul's. Now, it would be possible to rebut the first charge, if we could be sure (Harnack spoke of it as an assured fact) that Paul was acquitted and released after his imprisonment in Rome. The second charge is not decisive, and we can at least argue against the third. But when the linguistic charge is stated as Harrison stated it in *The Problem of the Pastorals* (1921)—with an almost bewildering wealth of statistics and graphs—the conservative reply looks like so much special pleading. We might find reasons for the appearance of some 300 new words (out of a total of nearly 900); but how are we to explain the fact that 'the connective tissue' (particles, etc.—a very subtle test of style) is clearly not Paul's?

And yet who that has read it can doubt that, say, in II Tim. 4 we are listening to *echter Paulus*—the authentic Apostle? It is hard to dismiss as a Paulinist's inventing some of the *obiter dicta* ('I have fought a good fight, etc.') and many of the *personalia* ('Demas hath forsaken me') found in the Pastorals. It is things like these which make the hypothesis of fragments probable, and persuade most scholars to-day that some brief notes of Paul to Timothy and Titus fell into a later teacher's hands. With them to serve as nucleus (so E. F. Scott argues), he composed the Pastorals, issuing them in Paul's name—and not unreasonably. Did they not give effect to much of Paul's teaching, and did they not incorporate genuine notes of the Apostle?

II

The two big problems of provenance and destination which have exercised the critics in the last fifty years are:

(1) Who were 'the foolish Galatians'?
(2) Where did Paul write his Prison Epistles?

Fifty years ago Sir William Ramsay, fresh from archæologising in Asia Minor, boldly challenged the traditional view that the recipients of Galatians were the inhabitants of ethnographic Galatia—the ancient kingdom in the north with its capital in Ancyra. Paul's addressees, he argued, were the people of Pisidian Antioch, Iconium, Lystra and Derbe whom he had evangelised on his first tour (Acts 13-14), i.e. the people living in the southern part of the *Roman province* of Galatia. So began a controversy as heated as any ever waged over the site of Mons Graupius or Hannibal's route across the Alps, and as late as 1911 Ramsay and Moffatt were crossing furious swords on the matter.

The question was: Did Paul use the word 'Galatia' ethnographically or politically? If, with Lightfoot at your back, you were a North Galatianist, you interpreted 'the Galatian region' in Acts 16.6 and 18.23 as the ancient kingdom of the Gauls in the north, and argued that since, in Acts, Pisidia, Lycaonia, etc., are geographical terms, so must Galatia be too. If you followed Ramsay, you argued that these passages in Acts described the part of Phrygia within the Roman province of Galatia, and held that, as Paul generally talks in terms of Roman provinces, Galatia must mean the Roman province. And there were many other ancillary arguments on both sides.

What has been the issue of the controversy? In Germany the opinion of critics has been divided. Although the veteran Zahn was an early convert to Ramsay's view, later scholars such as Lietzmann and Dibelius adhered to the old view. So far as Britain and America were concerned, the great majority declared themselves for Ramsay, and C. H. Turner dared to say in 1920 that Ramsay had 'swept the opposing theories from the field.'

Although we may not regard the matter as a *chose jugée*, we may judge it significant that most recent commentators on the letter (Emmet, Burton, W. L. Knox, Blunt, Dow and Duncan) think Ramsay is right and that, as J. A. Findlay says, 'all those who know the geography of Asia Minor well are South Galatianists to a man.'

Where did Paul write his Prison Epistles? In Rome? In Caesarea? Or in Ephesus? Tradition says Rome. Not many have favoured Caesarea. But what about Ephesus? In 1900 Lisco of Berlin plumped for Ephesus. Deissmann gave the new theory his support.[1] And in 1929 Dr. G. S. Duncan of St. Andrews produced a full-dress exposition of it in his book, *St. Paul's Ephesian Ministry*. It was obviously an issue of capital importance; for, if established, we should have to revise our whole picture of Paul's spiritual pilgrimage and perhaps write off as illusory those developments in doctrine detected in his letters by scholars from Sabatier to C. H. Dodd.

Prima facie, the theory seems improbable. Does not Philippians expressly refer to 'the saints of Caesar's household' and 'the Praetorian Guard'? But when we learn that the Greek *praitorion* means simply 'Government House' and that there were many such in the Roman Empire, and that 'Caesar's household' was a sort of Imperial Civil Service, of which (as we know from inscriptions) there were representatives in Ephesus, we are not so sure. Our confidence receives another blow when we ask ourselves: Is it likely that the ten or so friends named in the Prison Epistles *all* followed him to Rome?

At this point we may rightly object that Acts says nothing of an imprisonment in Ephesus.[2] True, but Acts is a far from complete account of Paul's life (see II Cor. 11.23ff.), and odd bits of evidence—'in prisons oft' (II Cor. 11.23), 'I fought with wild beasts in Ephesus' (I Cor. 15.32), the terrible 'affliction in Asia'

[1] *St. Paul*, 222.

[2] But your guide in the city of Ephesus to-day will point you to a square tower, standing on a slight elevation, as 'the prison of St. Paul.' How did the tradition arise?

(II Cor. 1.8), Andronicus and Junias 'my fellow prisoners' (Rom. 16.7)—plus some extra-canonical evidence (of which the chief is the Marcionite Prologue's claim that Colossians was written from Ephesus), certainly lend colour to Duncan's thesis. Add to this what Duncan calls 'the great argument'—that the Ephesian theory provides a much likelier setting for some or all of the Prison Epistles (for example, Ephesus, only 100 miles distant, is a much nearer place of refuge for the runaway Onesimus than Rome, at least 800 miles across the Sea).

How has the new hypothesis been received? Only one or two scholars (e.g. Michaelis of Germany) have gone all the way with Duncan. But if C. H. Dodd rejects the theory *in toto*,[1] most critics have pronounced it 'far from impossible,' and many think that the case for assigning Philippians to Ephesus is good. (If Luke in Acts had given us any hint that he was with Paul in Ephesus, we might assign Colossians and Philemon to Ephesus also; but since Luke, who figures among those who send greetings from Paul's prison in these letters, was with Paul in Rome, we must have grave hesitations here.) On the whole issue some will prefer the testimony of tradition; but the debate is still very much alive, and many of us will never feel quite confident when we speak of Philippians as Paul's 'swan-song' from his Roman prison.

Two other literary problems must be treated briefly. One is the destination of Rom. 16. In the last half-century many, with some reason, have regarded it as a separate letter sent to Ephesus. Here, as in the case of the Prison Epistles, C. H. Dodd prefers Rome.[2] Some evidence that Romans circulated in two recensions has evoked much discussion. Kirsopp Lake thought that an original circular letter of fourteen chapters was later lengthened into sixteen by St. Paul when he wrote to Rome. The commoner view has been that an original sixteen were cut down by

---

[1] *Rylands Bulletin*, January, 1934.

[2] But the fact that in P 45, our earliest Pauline codex (published in 1935), the Doxology (Rom. 16.25–7 in the A.V.) stands after 15.33 is evidence for those who assign Chapter 16 to Ephesus on other grounds.

someone for liturgical or doctrinal reasons. But the most convincing suggestion has been that of T. W. Manson:[1] Paul (he thinks) may have made *two* copies of Romans, sending the original one —consisting of 1–15—to Rome, and the second one—consisting of 1–16—to Ephesus. So, at one blow, he would clear up both our problems.

Is II Corinthians a unity? Last century Hausrath and Kennedy taught us that the abrupt change of tone beginning at II Cor. 10.1 proved 10–13 to be part of another letter, probably 'the severe letter' which came between the writing of I Corinthians and II Cor. 1–9. This theory still has many supporters, if it has no MS. evidence behind it. But Allan Menzies, who wrote a fine commentary on the Epistle in 1912, and Hans Lietzmann, who wrote in 1931, would have none of it. A sleepless night between the writing of 9 and 10, Lietzmann said, was explanation enough. Moreover, as he pointed out, Paul elsewhere ends with similar outbursts. But the break is very inartistic? True, replies Lietzmann, *'Das war freilich nicht "klug", aber der echte Paulus.'*[2] So, maintaining the integrity of the letter, we may believe that in 1–9 Paul addressed the church in Corinth, in 10–13 his enemies.[3]

III

Looking back on these fifty years, what are the contributions to Pauline studies which spring instantly to mind?

There have been 'lives,' of course, to do for our generation what Conybeare and Howson or Dean Farrar did for theirs: Paterson Smyth's admirable little book for beginners, David Smith's much bigger *Life and Letters of St. Paul*, A. D. Nock's *multum in parvo* on *St. Paul* in the Home University Library, and many more. Deissmann himself did much in his *St. Paul* to show us the real Paul when we were in danger of equating him with

---

[1] *Rylands Bulletin*, November, 1948. The whole discussion is very illuminating.

[2] *An die Korinther*, 139.

[3] In his *Chapters in a Life of Paul* (1950), John Knox has produced a new and startling chronology of Paul's life, based chiefly on the data in the letters, and largely rejecting the testimony of Acts. The present writer finds this part of Knox's able book unconvincing.

'the paper St. Paul of our Western libraries.' The Apostle threw his spell over two of our finest classical scholars: Sir William Ramsay, whose *St. Paul the Traveller and Roman citizen* revivified the missionary journeying of the Apostle, and T. R. Glover, whose *Paul of Tarsus* was only less refreshing than his study of Jesus. And Dean Inge wrote an essay on St. Paul the man which is already a classic. Nor did the Epistles fail to find great commentators: Johannes Weiss on I Corinthians, Burton on Galatians, and C. H. Dodd on Romans. Add to these great books from Germany and elsewhere which lit up the apostolic age or some important aspect of Paul's thought, which always stimulated, if they did not command our complete consent: Bousset's *Kyrios Christos* (never, alas! translated), Weiss's *History of Primitive Christianity*, Schweitzer's *Mysticism of Paul the Apostle*, completed in 1929 'on the Ogowe steamer on the way to Lambarene,' and Klausner's *From Jesus to Paul*, produced amid the turbulence in Palestine.

Let us choose three of the salient problems which these books raised, and attempt to indicate the main answers.

IV

What was Paul, a Hebrew of the Hebrews or a Hellenist of the Hellenists? This problem exercised our scholars mightily in the first two decades of this century.

That Paul availed himself here and there of Stoic terms such as 'conscience' or Stoic ideas such as that of 'the inner law,' as his dialectic sometimes reminds us of the Stoic diatribes—this was not new to us, this we might have expected in one who hailed from Tarsus, a Stoic centre. The matter became serious when in the early years of the century, Reitzenstein, Bousset and others[1] began to assert that Paul's whole conception of Christianity owed much to the pagan mystery religions which flourished rankly in the Graeco-Roman world of Paul's time, and offered salvation to many sick souls in fear of Fate, the malefic influence of the stars, annihilation and their like. The charge was that Paul (or, as

[1] The Englishman, Kirsopp Lake, was an apt pupil. See his *Landmarks in the History of Early Christianity*.

Bousset put it, some predecessors of his in Antioch) had changed Christ and Primitive Christianity into a full-blown mystery cult —'a generalised blend of Attis, Osiris and Mithras (three popular cult gods), wearing as a not too-well-fitting mask the features of Jesus of Nazareth.'[1] Paul might testify that to the Greeks his gospel was mere 'foolishness,' but Reitzenstein and others knew better. It was not merely a matter of Paul's having borrowed odd words from the mysteries: his mysticism, his doctrine of baptism as a dying and rising with Christ, his sacramental conception of the Eucharist, his worship of Jesus as 'Lord'—all sprang from the same source, the Greek mysteries. They did not stop to consider that their knowledge of these mysteries was really very scanty, that all this amazing transmogrification of the gospel must have taken place within twenty years, that, if Paul derived his message from his environment, he did what no other missionary has ever done—borrowed his gospel from the people among whom he worked.

Looking back on the whole thing now, one wonders how Reitzenstein and others managed to 'sell' their hypothesis to so many. Had they completely forgotten not only Paul's own claims, but his manifest debt to the Old Testament, his rabbinical exegesis, his eschatology, his doctrine of God? In any event, other scholars were not slow to leap to Paul's defence. They did not deny that Paul sometimes used such words as 'salvation' or 'mystery' or 'lord' which the mystagogues also employed; but they did assert that he used them differently, and they flatly denied that Paul has turned a simple 'Galilean Gospel' into a cosmic drama of redemption modelled on the mysteries.

Writing in 1925, the German Robert Eisler explains how he had once accepted the Mystery hypothesis, but now considered it 'one of the most erroneous conclusions that have ever arisen in New Testament study.' And though his fellow Jew, Klausner, still clings to it, the whole theory has lost caste in the world of scholarship. Kennedy,[2] Schweitzer[3] and N. P. Williams have all

---

[1] N. P. Williams in *Essays Catholic and Critical*, 391.
[2] *St. Paul and the Mystery Religions* (1913).   [3] *Paul and His Interpreters* (1912).

subjected it to very damaging criticism. Anderson Scott, in his *Christianity according to St. Paul* (1927), dismissed the influence of Hellenism upon Paul's thought as 'negligible.' And in 1947 W. D. Davies, in his *St. Paul and Rabbinical Judaism*, showed at point after point how Paul, despite his apostleship to the Gentiles, 'remained, as far as was possible, a Hebrew of the Hebrews, and baptised his rabbinic heritage into Christ.'[1]

'The stronger a man's natural quality,' said John Oman, 'the more likely he is to remain racy of his native soil.' So it was with St. Paul. Though we cannot deny that Hellenism was one of his 'tutors unto Christ,' we may be very sure that the subsoil of Paul's thought remained Jewish to the very end.

V

Our second question has close connections with the first one. It is: what is the relation of Paul to Jesus? Or, as Arnold Meyer said, 'Who founded Christianity? Jesus or Paul?'

Many German monographs handled this question in the first two decades of the century. And indeed, so long as the liberal picture of Jesus was regarded as true, it was bound to be raised. It was clear (if we may be allowed the anachronism) that Paul did not believe in 'the liberal Jesus.' How then did the 'Christ-cult' of the Pauline writings arise?

Wrede[2] found the answer in current Jewish beliefs about a Heavenly Man. Before Paul became a Christian (he said) he believed in a heavenly Messiah. At his conversion all he did was to transfer to Jesus the conceptions he already had of this heavenly Christ. His Christology really owed next to nothing to the historic figure of Jesus. Others, as we have seen, found a Greek answer. It was under the influence of the mystery religions that Paul turned Jesus into a redeemer God.

In any case, whichever explanation was preferred, Paul was really 'the villain of the piece.' It was he who radically changed

[1] E. R. Goodenough's recent attempt in his *By Light, Light* (1935) to prove the existence of a Hellenistic-Jewish mystery religion to which Paul may have been indebted, has not persuaded the experts.

[2] See his *Paul* (Eng. Tr., 1907).

the character of Christianity by turning a purely human Jesus into a supernatural Christ. Once this conclusion was drawn, it was an easy step to the next one, that Paul was the real founder of Christianity.

If few scholars to-day level this grave charge at St. Paul, what has made them revise their opinions?

First, Schweitzer and others showed the liberal Jesus to be a figment of the critics' imagination.

Second, the rediscovery of the eschatology in the Gospels—and in particular the better understanding of the Kingdom of God which we associate with Dodd and others—gave new and vast dimensions to the central Figure in the Gospel story. It confronted us with One who knew Himself to be the all-decisive Person at a supreme crisis in God's dealings with men.

Third, scholars like Denney who studied the self-revelation of Jesus in the Synoptic Gospels, recalled us to a Person who knew Himself to be the Son of God in a unique and lonely sense. We began to see that the Christology of Jesus Himself revealed One who was not unworthy to bear the weight of the lofty claims which St. Paul made for Him.

Fourth, the gulf which had seemed to yawn between St. Paul and the Primitive Church was well-nigh bridged. Fifty years ago a sharp contrast between Paul's creed and the creed of the Primitive Church was almost a dogma of critical orthodoxy. All that is changed now. We have begun to discover how much Paul owed theologically to his Christian predecessors.[1] We have learned that the *kerygma*[2] which he preached did not differ essentially from that of the earliest apostolic preachers (cf. I Cor. 15.11, 'Whether then it be I or they, so we preach and so ye believed'). To be sure, it fell to Paul (e.g. in Colossians) to explore the fact of Christ in ways that never came within the horizon of the original Jerusalem Apostles; but there is no record that they ever disagreed on the capital issue of Christology. If Paul

[1] See my book, *Paul and His Predecessors,* and J. Weiss, *The History of Primitive Christianity.*

[2] C. H. Dodd, *The Apostolic Preaching.*

called Jesus 'Lord' and set Him on the divine side of reality, so did they. If Paul acknowledged Jesus' name to be the only saving name under heaven, and knew that one day he must stand before Him as Judge, so did those who were 'in Christ' before him.

All these discoveries have helped to clear Paul of the charge of being the arch-corrupter of the Gospel. As Vidler puts it in his recent book, 'The idea is now discredited among scholars (though it popularly persists) that beneath the surface of the Gospels we can unearth a purely human prophet of the divine Fatherhood and human brotherhood, who was transformed by St. Paul into a supernatural Saviour.'[1] We are realising that to separate Jesus from Paul is 'as absurd as to explain the movements of the planets without reference to the sun.' We are returning to a firmly held conclusion of our forefathers that few, if any, of Jesus' interpreters saw more deeply into the secret of what He did and was than Paul of Tarsus.

VI

Let us take as our final question: What did Paul find in Christ and the Gospel? It will raise the whole problem of Paulinism and it will enable us to notice some recent trends in Pauline interpretation.

(1) The answer of traditional Protestantism has been: 'Justification by faith.' So Luther judged, and in his hand the doctrine—

> *became a trumpet, whence he blew*
> *Soul-animating strains.*

Our modern interpreters do not agree. 'That the so-called doctrine of justification is so prominent,' observes Deissmann, 'has less an inner than an outer cause. The hard fight against the Judaisers and the Law compelled Paul thereto.' 'Only a fragment' from something bigger is Schweitzer's verdict. Justification 'is a subsidiary crater, which was formed within the rim of the main crater—the mystical doctrine of redemption through being in Christ.' And W. D. Davies, declaring that its prominence in Paul is due to polemical necessities, describes it as 'one metaphor

[1] *Christian Belief*, 48.

among many others employed by Paul to describe his deliverance through Christ.'

This last verdict seems the best. Justification is only, for Paul, an initial step on the way to salvation. And it is only in Romans and Galatians, where he clearly has the Judaisers and salvation by works in his eye, that the doctrine bulks large.

(2) The answer often given in modern times to our question can be put in three words: union with Christ. 'The religion of Paul,' says Deissmann, 'is quite simple. It is communion with Christ.' 'Union with Christ,' declares H. R. Mackintosh, 'is a brief name for all that the Apostles meant by salvation.' And Schweitzer's book on Paul's theology[1] is one long study of 'redemption through being in Christ' (which he invites us to understand in 'a quasi-physical way').

What does 'being in Christ' mean? Deissmann (who traces Hellenistic influence here) says that the formula[2] describes 'the most intimate fellowship imaginable of the Christian with the living spiritual Christ.' Just as the air we breathe is in us and fills us, and yet we also live and breathe in the air, so is Paul's fellowship with Christ.

Who can doubt that this is a true account of the matter, so far as it goes? But does it go far enough? Does it do full justice to Paul's usage of the great phrase?

Interpreters since Deissmann have rightly noted that the formula has often a clearly corporate connotation, so that to be in Christ also means to be included in 'the corporate personality which is manifested in the Church.' To choose one example out of many, Rom. 8.1: 'There is now no condemnation to those who are in Christ Jesus.' Being in Christ, as Flew says, carries with it the idea of membership in the *Ecclesia*, which is His Body. 'Christ and His People,' says G. S. Duncan, 'form a corporate fellowship, so that to be in Christ means to be a member of that religious fellowship which draws its very life from Christ.' In other words, Pauline mysticism is no flight of the alone to the Alone.

---

[1] *The Mysticism of Paul the Apostle* (1931).
[2] It occurs 155 times in Paul's Epistles (excluding the Pastorals).

To be in Christ, as W. D. Davies says, is a social concept; it is to have discovered the true community. And when a man by faith and baptism enters that community, he enters mystically into the virtue of all that Christ has done for him by dying and rising again.[1]

We may welcome all this new light on what Paul means by 'being in Christ' without being, however, quite convinced that it is the best answer to the question with which we started.

(3) The wisest answer is to be found in Anderson Scott's *Christianity according to St. Paul*, perhaps the best book on Pauline theology this half-century has produced.[2] What Paul found in Christ and the Gospel was 'salvation.' It was that for which his contemporaries, both Jewish and Greek, were seeking. It was that which Paul found in Christ and the Gospel. 'The Gospel,' he said, 'is the power of God unto salvation'—God's divine force for saving men. This salvation, as Paul expounds it, has three aspects. It is a past event, a present experience, and a future hope. As a past event, it rested on 'the finished work' of Christ, and might be called 'redemption,' 'justification' and 'reconciliation.' All three were metaphors for the initial stage in the salvation offered by God in Christ. To it man's right response was faith, of whose reality baptism was the seal. But salvation is also, for Paul, a present experience. It means to be 'in Christ,' to live by the power of the Spirit the life that is life indeed, in the fellowship of the new People of God, the Church, which is Christ's Body. This new life is one of sonship, its finest fruit is love, and its appointed nourishment is the Lord's Supper.

But, finally, for Paul, salvation is a future hope. It can only be realised in its completeness when, with Christ's *Parousia* and the consummation of all things, sin and death are overcome and the redeemed, in heaven, beholding God and Christ face to face, enjoy the last and uttermost beatitude.

[1] 'To be "in Christ",' says John Knox (*op. cit.*, 158), 'is to be a member of the ultimate eschatological order, the divine community of love, proleptically present and partially realised in the Church, whose spirit is the very Spirit of God and the very presence of the risen Christ.'

[2] Another similar—and excellent—book is Sydney Cave's *The Gospel of St. Paul* (1928). Dr. Cave brings his own missionary insights to the understanding of the Apostle.

So to regard Paul's theology is to see it in its true perspective. It is to set 'justification by faith' and 'being in Christ' in their proper places in his scheme of thought. It is to glimpse something of the true width and grandeur of Christianity according to St. Paul. And all of it lies latent in the first verse of the fifth chapter to the Romans: 'Therefore being justified by faith, we have peace with God through our Lord Jesus Christ, by whom also we have access by faith into this grace wherein we stand, and rejoice in hope of the glory of God.'

VII

No account of Pauline studies in the twentieth century would be complete without a word of epilogue on the rediscovery of Paul the man. It was Chrysostom who said: 'Though he was an Apostle, he was also a man.' Our twentieth-century scholars have disinterred the living man from the dead weight of Paulinism under which, at the end of the last century, he was in grave danger of being smothered. Nothing better on this subject has been written than Dean Inge's classic essay (*Outspoken Essays, First Series*): 'In the nineteenth century,' he says, 'Paul was obscured behind Paulinism. His letters were studied as treatises on systematic theology. . . . The name of the Apostle came to be associated with angular and frigid disquisitions which were rapidly losing their connexion with vital religion. It has been left for scholars of the present century to give us a picture of St. Paul as he really was—a man much nearer to George Fox or John Wesley than to Origen or Calvin; the greatest of missionaries and pioneers, and only incidentally a great theologian.' The late T. R. Glover also did much to humanise the Apostle and make him less of a parchment saint or a Teutonic professor of systematic theology. But it was the men who went back to study the Anatolian lands where Paul's work was done, Ramsay and Deissmann, who did most to re-create for us the living man. These two (with their later follower, H. V. Morton) delivered Paul 'from his eighth imprisonment in the paper bondage of Paulinism,' put him back into his proper *milieu*, 'the world of the olive tree,' and helped us to see him as he really was: a small, dynamic, intrepid man moving ceaselessly among the cities of the Levant, raising either a riot or a revival wherever he went, working with his own hands to keep himself alive for his great task, writing non-literary letters (not stiff epistles) to his spiritual children in Thessalonika, Philippi, Corinth, Galatia; a man dominated by a great ambition to preach the Gospel in Rome; a man to whom Christ meant more than Christology and God than the doctrine of God; a man of almost polar opposites—physically weak yet immensely tough; utterly humble yet also utterly sure of the high role God had called him to play; tenderly affectionate, yet also (when moved) stern, wrathful, volcanic; subject to depression yet also (the true mark of the saint) 'radiant amidst the storm and stress of life' and invincibly sure of God and Christ and the unseen things; a man of his time, a Pharisee captured by Christ, full of rabbinical dialectic, no sex-equalitarian, believing in mystical visions and 'tongues,' in evil spirits, in a three-storied world; a man speaking and writing the international Greek of the age with a Semitic accent, mixing with all sorts and conditions of men, Jewish and Gentile, and undergoing such hardships and persecutions as few men in history have undergone; yet withal never for one moment doubting Him in whom he had believed and persuaded that He was able to keep that which He had committed unto him until the great Day of the Lord.

This is the man who stands before us in the pages of Deissmann and Ramsay.[1] Beside him the other Apostles seem almost shadows. 'Alone he breathes and lives,' says Dean Inge, quoting Homer (on the seer Teiresias among the dead), 'while they flit as shadows.' Paul the man from Tarsus, Pharisee of the Pharisees, *Civis Romanus*, Apostle to the Gentiles; first of Christian mystics, most dynamic of Christian missionaries, bond-servant of Jesus Christ; the man who, under God, did more than any other to set Christ's 'hallowed fire' blazing in the world, the most illustrious name in the roll-call of the saints.

[1] There is a very discerning chapter on Paul the man in John Knox's *Chapters in a Life of Paul* (1950), 89–107.

VII

Johannine Studies: 1. The Fourth Gospel

✳

IT is customary among critics to speak of 'the problem of the Fourth Gospel.' The phrase is misleading. The Johannine problem is polygonal. It is not simply, Did John son of Zebedee write the Gospel, and when, and where, and why? The problem branches out endlessly. Is the Gospel a unity? Do we have it in its original order? Does an Aramaic original glimmer through its Greek dress? Did the Fourth Evangelist know the Synoptists? How far do the discourses in the Gospel reproduce the mind of Jesus? And where do history and reflection begin and end in the Gospel?

These questions form the staple of the Johannine debate. It began long before the twentieth century, but it has been continued—and advanced—in the last fifty years. In this chapter we propose to pick out a dozen significant contributions to it from British and from non-British scholars during the last half-century and to indicate present trends.

I

We begin with British work. At the beginning of the century most British scholars, led by William Sanday, still clung to the apostolic authorship, and were ready to use the Gospel almost equally with the Synoptists as a source for the life and teaching of Jesus. Perhaps the ablest book of this kind was the Unitarian James Drummond's *Character and Authorship of the Fourth Gospel* (1903). Drummond devotes only sixty pages to the 'character'; the remaining five hundred are spent on 'authorship.' He finds the external evidence all on one side, and most of the internal in harmony with it. Judging the difficulties insufficient to weigh down the balance, he decides in favour of apostolic authorship.

If Drummond's book ably stated the conservative view, E. F. Scott's *Fourth Gospel* (1906) brilliantly expounded the advanced. Quietly assuming with Continental scholars the non-apostolic authorship and a date at the beginning of the second century, he plunges straight into a lucid exposition of the Fourth Evangelist's aims and theology. The Gospel (he insists) was designed to interpret Jesus and His message to the Hellenistic world. To understand it, we must recall the forces facing the Church in Asia at the end of the first century: the Christian controversy with hostile Jewry ('the Jews'), infiltrating Gnosticism, the extravagant claims being made for the Baptist in some quarters, etc. The clue to the Logos doctrine is to be sought in Philo, the Alexandrian Jew. For 'John,' Jesus is supremely the Son of God who came to reveal the unseen Father and give men the secret of eternal life. His work is at once a historical record and a record of spiritual facts. He sets forth the Jesus of history in terms of the Christ of faith. So he who was not a contemporary of Jesus shows us the Jesus who is our eternal contemporary.

A year after Scott's book appeared the Roman Church's Biblical Commission, alarmed at the rising tide of modernism, instructed the faithful thus: 'It is no longer a question of knowing if it had as author the Beloved Disciple, John, son of Zebedee. This point is fixed by ecclesiastical tradition.' How pained the Commissioners must have been to read the account of the Gospel which one of their own communion, Von Hügel, contributed in 1911 to the *Encyclopædia Britannica* (11th ed.). For the good Baron's article, though profound, was far from orthodox. He found the author in a disciple of John the Elder, who was the Beloved Disciple, and thought that the Gospel, though drafted in A.D. 97, was not published till 120. Among its characteristics he discovered a tendency to handle history with considerable freedom, the mystic's love of double meanings, and 'the attempt to englobe the successiveness of man in the simultaneity of God.' Above all, he saw the Gospel as a great piece of allegorising, from Mary at Cana, representing 'faithful Israel,' to Christ's 'seamless robe,' symbol of the Church's unity.

About a decade later, when the 'Hellenists' seemed to be carrying all before them, the Semitic scholar, C. F. Burney, struck a notable blow on the other side. In the *Aramaic Origin of the Fourth Gospel* (1922) he piled linguistic argument upon argument to prove the thesis of his title. In sentence-structure, conjunctions, pronouns, verbs and negatives he found evidence for his view, and he produced examples of alleged mistranslations of an underlying Aramaic original. The argument about his thesis (later supported by Torrey) is not yet over, but few have gone all the way with him. Yet if Burney has not convinced the experts that 'John' wrote his Gospel in Aramaic, he has persuaded most of them that Aramaic must have been his *mother-tongue*.

Our last two British books are both commentaries. The first, J. H. Bernard's two-volumed work in *The International Critical Commentary* series, appeared posthumously in 1928. It is in the Anglican tradition on the Fourth Gospel—learned, sober, conservative. To be sure, Bernard surrenders the apostolic authorship, but he does the next best thing by ascribing the Gospel to John the Elder and finding the witness of John the Apostle (the Beloved Disciple) behind the book. He assumes dislocations in the text, admits indirect influence from Philo on the thought, but will have nothing to do with those who find allegory writ large in the Gospel. Take it all in all, Bernard's is perhaps the soundest British commentary in this century.

Our last book, Sir Edwyn Hoskyns' *The Fourth Gospel*, published posthumously in 1940, has a certain inchoateness which the writer, had he lived, would have done much to remove. It is also marred in places by an over-subtle, 'Origen-esque' exegesis.[1] But his approach is certainly the right one. Theologically conceived documents should be treated as theology, and in the Fourth Gospel he finds the solution to the riddle of the first three. The Synoptists raise problems which they never fully answer—

[1] E.g. John 19.30, παρέδωκε τὸ πνεῦμα: 'He handed over the Spirit' to the faithful waiting below.

for example, the enigma of Jesus, a figure inexplicable by the ordinary standards of humanity. John supplies the key. His Gospel shows us the *wholeness* lying hidden in the Marcan episodes and the sayings of Q. For John sees the story of Jesus *sub specie aeternitatis,* and his theme is 'the non-historical which makes sense of history.' There is in the Fourth Gospel a tension, a tension between spirit and flesh, between God and man, a tension focused at the point where man and time meet God and eternity, where we are confronted by Jesus the Son of man— the Son of God. Jesus Christ is the place where God breaks into our world-order, and His life, death and Resurrection are really the conclusive utterance of the Word of God to man.

It should be clear, even from this inadequate summary, that Hoskyns, for all his defects, has shown us 'a more excellent way' of approaching the profoundest of all the Gospels.

I I

It is, of course, chronologically wrong to start with British work and then go on to German. Here, as in so many other fields, Germany led the van. And how far that van was 'ahead' of the British rearguard at the turn of the century, the article on the Gospel in *The Encyclopædia Biblica* by P. W. Schmiedel (1901) shows.

Schmiedel finds Irenaeus in error. The John of Asia, of whom he wrote, was John the Elder, not the Apostle. But the Fourth Evangelist was neither Apostle nor Elder. He was an anonymous Christian of Asia who wrote after A.D. 132 (John 5.43 refers to Bar Cochba's revolt!). His Gospel has little claim to historical value. A book which begins by calling Jesus the Logos of God and ends by representing a cohort of Roman soldiers as falling to the ground at the majesty of His appearance ought not (he says) to be treated as history. Its true merit is its masterly reinterpretation of Christianity for cultured people in the second century and for Christians of all ages who boggle at the traditional dogmas. On one point Schmiedel was conservative—'the Fourth

Gospel is like the seamless coat, not to be divided, but to be taken as it is.'

Yet the seamless coat was in jeopardy, as our next book, Wellhausen's *Das Evangelium Johannes* (1908), shows. Wellhausen was one of many German critics at this time who sought, by analysing out the work of later redactors, to lay bare a Johannine *Grundschrift* (basic document). A discrepancy usually supplies the starting-point. Thus John 14.31, 'Arise, let us go hence,' has its immediate continuation in 18.1. *Ergo*, 15–17 are a redactor's interpolation. He admits that we cannot accurately sort out the various 'layers' in the Gospel, but is convinced that this is the right approach. About the Gospel's origin we can know little, but it is certainly late.

We may skip a decade and take another important German book, Johannes Weiss's *Urchristentum*, completed after his death by Rudolf Knopf and published in 1917. Again we are invited to think of a *Grundschrift* on which a redactor has been busy. Who was its writer? He was John of Ephesus *alias* John the Elder *alias* a Jerusalemite who had known Jesus *alias*—John Mark! After his death a devoted disciple enlarged the basic writing. 'John' builds on history, but aims to do much more. 'In the Incarnate One he gazes on the Exalted One, and he animates the portrait of the Exalted One by the picture of the Incarnate.' The speeches of Jesus have all passed through the alembic of the Evangelist's original mind; but he 'often draws the brief themes of his discourses from the tradition, and twines his own meditations round and round these nuclear words.' What are the sources of Johannine Christianity? The Synoptic Gospels, of course. Paulinism? Yes, but Paulinism purged of its rabbinism. Judaism too, but Judaism of a Philonian sort. All these, but above all the Christian experience of a great mystic.

Would the Fourth Gospel yield anything to the form critic's researches? Hans Windisch, who wrote three notable essays on the Gospel between 1923 and 1927,[1] thought that it would. A

---

[1] *Der Johanneische Erzählungsstil* (1923); *Johannes und die Synoptiker* (1926); *Die Fünf Johanneischen Parakletsprüche* (1927).

study of 'John's' narrative style revealed to him different **kinds** of narrative: detailed dramatic stories like the Woman of Samaria; stories-cum-controversies like the Impotent Man of Bethesda; and little series of related scenes like the winning of Christ's Disciples in 1.35-51. Then he turned to the old problem of the relation between John and the Synoptists, but reached a new conclusion. John's attitude to his predecessors might be described in words from his own book: 'All that came before me are thieves and robbers'! In other words, John wrote not to supplement the Synoptists, but to supplant them. His last study was of the five Paraclete sayings in the Gospel. These, he argued, form a unity and are intruders into the Farewell Discourses where they interrupt the sequence of thought. We should regard them as insertions and isolate them for separate study.

The last German contribution we shall notice is Rudolf Bultmann's commentary on the Gospel (*Das Johannes-Evangelium*), which appeared in 1937-41. A hundred years before, Baur could not find it possible to date the Gospel earlier than 170. The discovery of the C. H. Roberts fragment convinces Bultmann that its date must be before A.D. 100. Yet Bultmann shows that he is still suffering from 'the Mandaean fever' which afflicted German scholarship in the nineteen-twenties, following the discovery of the Mandaean scriptures, for he asserts the Mandaean origin of much of John's thought. He also traces the hand of an ecclesiastical redactor and believes that the text has suffered much dislocation. The interesting thing about this book is that Bultmann believes the Evangelist to have used three sources: (*a*) a sayings collection, probably originally in Aramaic, to be distinguished by its rhythmical style, its antithetic statements, and its 'I am' sayings; (*b*) a miracle stories source; and (*c*) another source, independent of the Synoptic tradition though parallel to it, which supplied some of his narratives as well as his Passion story. From Schmiedel to Bultmann is only forty years; but we may surely talk of progress in Fourth Gospel study when the most radical critic alive can now speak of something very like a Johannine Q!

In this survey there are inevitably great gaps. Space will not allow reference to be made to the work of Abbott in England or Loisy in France. But we cannot conclude our list of a dozen contributors to the debate without mentioning the prolific writings of Professor B. W. Bacon of Yale. (His two biggest books on the Fourth Gospel were *The Fourth Gospel in Research and Debate* (1910) and *The Gospel of the Hellenists* (1933); but the student will find his views summarised in Chapter IX of *The Making of the New Testament* (1912).

At the beginning of the century Bacon was ready to discern three hands in the Gospel—those of John the Beloved Disciple, the Elder, and the author of the Appendix. Ten years later he had got rid of the Apostle and the Elder, and found the author in an Ephesian of the second century, who took Paul as the model for his portrait of the Beloved Disciple. Bacon found textual dislocations to be widespread, and detected everywhere the hand of a redactor who lived in Rome about A.D. 150. In his last book he argued that a form of Samaritan Gnosticism called forth the polemic in the Fourth Gospel.

Bacon was a brilliant and ingenious man, but few of his speculations have won acceptance. His own view of the Gospel may be summed up thus. The Gospel is a treatise whose primary aim is not fact but truth. Its discourses are theology, not history. Though he knew the Synoptic tradition, the Fourth Evangelist transformed its miracles into symbols, its sayings into allegories, in order to produce an interpretation of the Person and Work of the God-man. His 'heaped-up tangle of anecdote, dialogue and allegory' is really an application of Paul's doctrine of the Incarnation couched in terms of the Stoic Logos theory. Knowing little (like St. Paul) of the Jesus of history, he nevertheless stands revealed as 'the truest expositor of the heart of Christ.'

III

Fifty years ago discussion of this Gospel commonly began with the questions of authorship, date and provenance. When you had answered them, you turned to the other questions. Nowadays—

witness Hoskyns' Introduction—discussion generally starts with the other questions. However, in this summary of recent trends, it will be convenient to begin in the old way.

When was the Gospel written? We can answer this question more confidently than our predecessors fifty years ago. The discovery of a fragment of the Gospel in Egypt which the experts are sure cannot be later than A.D. 125, makes a date for St. John later than A.D. 100 highly unlikely.

The critics of the last half-century have not quarrelled much about the Gospel's place of origin. Though a few (Burney, Bultmann and T. W. Manson) have thought that it may have had a connexion with Antioch, and one (J. K. Sanders) has hazarded Alexandria, most accept Percy Gardner's title for it, 'the Ephesian Gospel.'

Who wrote the Gospel? It is commonly supposed that the answers to this question are almost as many as the critics themselves. It is well, therefore, to remember that on certain aspects of it there is general agreement:

(1) That the writer was a Jew—probably an Aramaic-speaking Jew of Palestine—who lived in a Hellenistic environment; and

(2) that if he was not 'the Seer' of Revelation—a conclusion reached by Dionysius in the third century—he was almost certainly 'the Elder' of the Epistles.

It is when we go on from there that the diversity really begins; but, ultimately, there are only three possible answers:

(a) The conservative answer: John son of Zebedee.

(b) The radical answer: an unknown Christian of Asia.

(c) The 'mediating' answer: a disciple of the Apostle John.

One of the big differences between 1900 and 1950 is that very few critics are now prepared to defend the *direct* apostolic authorship. When that is said, we must go on to say that the conservative position does not look nearly so indefensible as it did, say, twenty years ago. To begin with, the critics are realising that the evidence for the early martyrdom of John the Apostle is both late and slight. Second, after all the conjectures have been heard, the likeliest view is that which identifies the Beloved Disciple with the Apostle John. And, in the third place, if the Fourth Gospel was written before the end of the first century when many persons were still alive who could confirm or contradict it, the certificate of authorship in 21.24, written evidently by persons of authority, can hardly be dismissed as a late forger's attempt to authenticate his work. Ultimately, it is the divergencies between the Johannine and the Synoptic accounts of Jesus' Ministry and Teaching (though these, as Temple showed,[1] are often much exaggerated) which make us hesitate about accepting the conservative answer.

The difficulty about the radical answer is not only that it rejects good tradition (like that of Irenaeus), but that it fails to explain the marks of the eye-witness (cf. 1.14), the apostolic authority of the book (well brought out by Scott Holland[2]), the excellent Palestinian geography and the undoubted Aramaisms, and the patently good tradition (Goguel's point) which the Gospel preserves in many places.

So the theory which comes nearest to satisfying all the conditions is one which ascribes the Gospel to a disciple of the Apostle. This is, in fact, the answer given by most British scholars in the last fifty years; and many of them, not content with saying 'a disciple of the Apostle,' have named John the Elder, to whose existence Papias testifies, as the probable writer. If this be the truth, then the Gospel is, in Harnack's phrase, 'the Gospel of John (the Elder) according to John (the son of Zebedee).'

Is the Gospel a unity? Two or three decades ago German critics were busy turning the seamless robe of the Gospel into a patchwork quilt. The usual formula was a *Grundschrift* and several redactors. One scholar found traces of no less than seven hands in it. Unfortunately for the dissectors, most of their analyses were mutually self-destructive. Now, however, all this use of the

[1] *Readings in St. John's Gospel*, xxii.ff.
[2] *The Fourth Gospel* (1923).

critical knife has become suspect. *Grundschriften* are going out of
fashion. Stylistic studies leave a strong impression of literary
unity. R. H. Strachan (to take one example) once an avowed
'partitionist,' has written this recantation in the latest edition of
his commentary: 'I have found it necessary to join those who are
convinced that the Gospel is an essential unity.'[1] And, abroad,
Eduard Schweizer[2] and P. H. Menoud after applying linguistic
and other tests, have reached the same conclusion.

Do we have the Gospel in its original order? In the first two
or three decades of the century there was a craze for rearranging
the Gospel. (Readers of Moffatt's translation will recall how often
he transposes sections of the Gospel to what he calls their 'true'
positions.) This was not mere critical wilfulness. We cannot preclude the possibility of accidental dislocations in a parent manuscript of the Gospel. The leaves of an archetypal codex might
easily get disarranged. It is undeniable, too, that if we reverse the
order of Chapters 5 and 6, we apparently improve the geography
of Jesus' movements; and that if we put Chapters 15 and 16 at
13.31, we remove the inconcinnity caused by the appearance of
sixty verses of discourse after Jesus has said, 'Rise, let us go hence.'
Moreover, if we can go on to show that the passages we think
displaced are multiples of a common unit corresponding to the
number of letters on a papyrus codex leaf, the proposed reshuffling
becomes less open to the charge of arbitrariness. Much has been
attempted along these lines, as readers of the commentaries by
Macgregor and Bernard know; and one of the most piquant suggestions is that John 2.13–3.21 (the Cleansing of the Temple and
the Interview with Nicodemus) should follow 12.36—a trans-
position, at any rate, devoutly to be wished! Yet all such reshuffling implies that the twentieth-century critic knows what John
really intended—a big assumption. We must not confuse our
'feelings' about the right order with 'proof.' It is significant that
a number of recent scholars (Hoskyns, Dodd and Lightfoot) are
sceptical about dislocations.

[1] *The Fourth Gospel* (1941), v.
[2] In his *Ego Eimi* (1939).

Now let us take the problem of St. John and the Synoptists. Did John know the Synoptic Gospels? In 1927 Vincent Taylor[1] summed it up thus: 'Opinion is practically unanimous that the Evangelist used Mark; it is divided as to the use of Luke; and, on the whole, unfavourable to the writer's use of Matthew.' But in 1938 Gardner-Smith's *Saint John and the Synoptics* reopened the whole question. His case was (*a*) that when recounting the same incident John differs greatly from Mark; and (*b*) that striking verbal similarities (e.g. '*pistic* nard' in the story of the Anointing) between them are due to their independent borrowing from a common oral tradition. If Gardner-Smith has not convinced all critics, he has shown at least that the case for John's dependence on the Synoptics is weaker than we had supposed.

Let us consider next the background of the Gospel.

Every book shows traces somewhere of the world in which it was written and the spiritual winds blowing through it at the time. How much light can we shed on the spiritual background of the Fourth Gospel and the historical factors which helped to shape its distinctive theology? This is a problem which has continuously engaged researchers in the twentieth century.

It has long been recognised that Gnosticism was a factor in the religious *Umwelt* of the Fourth Gospel, and that the emphasis on the issue of 'blood and water' from our Lord's pierced side (19.34) and John's avoidance of the word *gnosis* indicate that he was alive to the perils of Gnosticism. But we have always to beware that we are not following false scents in this field. One such has been Mandaism.[2] The discovery of the sacred books of the Mandaeans, a sect claiming connexion with John the Baptist and still surviving in Iraq, led Bauer and Bultmann to find here a source for Johannine theology. Fuller study of this literature by Lietzmann and Burkitt shows that Mandaism is really a sort of Marcionite Gnosticism with an admixture of Nestorian Christianity.

There is much more to be said for the view that Alexandrian

---

[1] *Hibbert Journal*, July, 1927.
[2] *Manda* means 'knowledge.'

speculation of the type found in Philo had an indirect influence on Johannine theology. The thought behind the saying 'My Father worketh hitherto, and I work' has parallels in Philo, as his teaching about the Logos which distributes a heavenly food of the soul called manna finds echoes in the sixth chapter of the Fourth Gospel.

In recent years, however, it is to Judaism rather than Hellenism that scholars have been turning for light on the Gospel's background. Abrahams, Burney, Odeberg and Schlatter have all argued that the polemical discourses of Jesus in Jerusalem reveal traits of thought and style best understood in the light of contemporary rabbinism.

And, of course, in any attempt to explain Johannine theology we cannot ignore Paulinism. The Johannine writings are later than the Pauline corpus, and emanate from a Pauline 'sphere of influence.' Not surprisingly, therefore, they show evidence of correspondences with Paul's theology. But there are also marked differences (see, for example, Anderson Scott's *Living Issues in the New Testament*), and we must always remember that much of what Paul and John have in common is really common apostolic Christianity, and not something of Paul's own inventing.

But, in the last resort, the central force behind the Gospel is not Philo, or even Paul, but Jesus Himself, Jesus drawing to Himself all that was best in the contemporary world of thought, Jesus as He lived and wrought in the soul of the Evangelist by the power of the promised Paraclete.

All our problems lead up in the end to the crucial ones of the historical value and essential meaning of the Gospel.

Before you can answer the question, How much history is there in the Fourth Gospel? you must settle your account with the prior one: What part do symbolism and allegory play in it? There have been times in the last fifty years when some of our scholars seemed bent on finding allegory everywhere, from the water-pots of Cana and the Samaritan Woman's five husbands to the seamless robe of Christ and the hundred and fifty-three fishes. Although Hoskyns makes free use of the allegorical method (for one example among many, see his comment on John 21.11)[1] the tendency of recent scholarship has been to find much more history and much less allegory in the Gospel. This is not to deny the element of symbolism—in the sense that for John the historical event is instinct with spiritual meaning. But if one may judge from recent British books such as Bernard's and Howard's, our scholars are much readier to insist that, if John has an eye for the deeper meaning of a Gospel incident (the cure of a blind man, the feeding of a multitude, or the effect of a lance-thrust), he always builds on what he believes to be real history. At point after point where John disagrees with the Synoptists, we have to stop and ask ourselves: 'Is it not conceivable that he may be right?' Indeed, if a count were taken on two pieces of Johannine historical testimony—his witness to an early Judean Ministry and the date of the Crucifixion—a majority of scholars would probably prefer to follow John. Now, if John be right on these two not unimportant matters, he has at least established a claim to an unprejudiced hearing on a great many others. T. W. Manson sums up the whole tendency thus: 'It is no longer possible to say, "If the Fourth Gospel contradicts the Synoptists, so much the worse for the Fourth Gospel." '[2]

In the same way the critics have begun to modify their views on the historical worth of the Johannine Discourses. The extreme view, that they are simply the Fourth Evangelists's inspired inventions, finds fewer and fewer advocates. Many Johannine sayings have direct or indirect Synoptic parallels. Drummond has collected dozens of short, pregnant utterances which, if they had first turned up in the Synoptic Gospels, would never have raised a critical eyebrow. Abrahams, the Jewish scholar, has declared his belief that 'the Gospel enshrines a genuine tradition of an aspect of Jesus' teaching which has not found a place in the Synoptics.' And, most astonishing of all, Bultmann has begun to talk of something very like a Johannine Q. These things have all worked for a

[1] *Op. cit.*, 661. 153, being the sum of the first 17 of the natural numbers, is therefore a triangular number! Most fishermen could find a simpler explanation.

[2] *Rylands Bulletin*, May, 1947.

much more conservative approach to the historical problem of the Discourses. Some have thought that the Platonic Dialogues furnish a good analogy. The Discourses preserve the thoughts of Jesus in a Johannine idiom just as the Dialogues enshrine the thoughts of Socrates in the words of Plato. A better analogy has been found in the Aramaic Targums which are often very free and interpretative expositions of Old Testament passages. Vincent Taylor comes near this view when he speaks of the Discourses as 'inspired airs composed on the basis of original themes.' But perhaps one of the Johannine sayings themselves—John 14.25f.—takes us as near the secret as anything else: (a) the words of Jesus—'These things have I spoken unto you'; (b) the illuminated memory of the disciples—'He shall bring to your remembrance all that I have said unto you'; and (c) the interpreting Spirit—'He shall teach you all things.'

Our last question is this: in the profound interlocking of history and theology which is the Gospel, what is it that the Fourth Evangelist did for his contemporaries—has done for us? That he set the teaching of Jesus free from the Jewish time-perspective of primitive Christianity by 'transposing the dialect of Jewish apocalyptic into the universal language of mystical fellowship'; that by his *Logos* doctrine he related the story of Christ to the best available thought of his time; and that by his teaching about the Spirit he gave to Christianity a charter of freedom, securing it from all false bondage to the past—these are W. F. Howard's claims for it,[1] and they cannot be gainsaid. The words which Browning set on the lips of the dying son of Zebedee also contain profound truth:

> *What first were guessed as points I now knew stars*
> *And named them in the Gospel I have writ.*

Claims and truths which only glimmer through the Synoptic record (the Messiahship of Jesus, his unique filial relationship to the Father, his purpose to found a new People of God, his promise of the Spirit, the mission to the Gentiles, to name only a few)

---

[1] *The Fourth Gospel in Recent Criticism and Interpretation*, 244.

shine out with wonderful clarity in the Fourth Gospel. But perhaps John's essential purpose is best suggested by some words of Hoskyns: 'He has so presented the "sensible" history of Jesus that his readers are confronted in that history, and precisely there, with what is beyond time and visible occurrence, with the veritable Word of God and with the veritable life of eternity.'[1]

Happily, the spiritual value of the Fourth Gospel does not stand or fall with the conclusions of the critics. Their opinions vary with the passing years, but the inherent power of the Gospel to comfort and upbuild the simple-hearted in his faith remains unchanged. It is still 'the text-book of the parish-priest and the inspiration of the straightforward layman.'[2] To a layman, Von Hügel, we will leave the last words: 'The greatness of the Gospel appears,' he says, 'in its inexhaustibly deep teaching concerning Christ's sheep and fold, the Father's drawing of souls to Christ; the dependence of knowledge as to Christ's doctrine upon the doing of God's will; the fulfilling of the commandment of love, as the test of true discipleship; eternal life begun even here and now; and God a Spirit, to be served in spirit and in truth.'[3]

[1] *The Fourth Gospel*, I, 4.   [2] Hoskyns, *op. cit.*, 6.   [3] *Op. cit.*

VIII

Johannine Studies: 2. The Epistles and Revelation

✳

THE Fourth Gospel is the *magnum opus* in the Johannine Library which, after St. Paul's letters, forms the most homogeneous literary and theological *bloc* in the New Testament. We have now to consider the opinions of our twentieth-century scholars on the remaining four books: the three Epistles linked with the name of John and the Apocalypse traditionally known as 'the Revelation of St. John the Divine.'

I

We start with the Epistles. *Prima facie,* we seem to have here a little tract and two brief letters written by the same man, designated in II and III John 'the Elder,' and obviously some venerable Church leader. I John, a pastoral homily of 105 verses, full of echoes of the Fourth Gospel, is evidently directed against some Christians who had become tainted with Gnosticism of a Docetic sort. II John, a miniature of I John, is addressed to a local church cryptically styled 'the elect lady.' III John, a confidential note to Gaius, bespeaks a worthy reception for some Christian missionaries and warns against a local ecclesiastic, Diotrephes, who had flouted the writer's authority. The general opinion has been that all three letters are by the same hand, that they were written in Asia near the end of the first century, and that possibly 'the Elder' was the Presbyter John, who may have been a sort of bishop in Ephesus, the mother-church of Asia.

Few have doubted that II and III John are by the same hand

as I John. The real question has been whether I John is by the same hand that wrote the Fourth Gospel.

In 1903 Denney[1] stated the commonly accepted view with his wonted trenchancy: 'If these two books [the Fourth Gospel and I John] cannot be ascribed to the same hand, literary criticism is bankrupt.' A. E. Brooke's excellent I.C.C. commentary on the Epistles (1912) affirmed the common authorship. B. H. Streeter[2] in 1924 found 'the minute differences' between the Gospel and I John far less than those which divide the earlier, middle, and captivity Epistles of Paul, and ascribed the Gospel and three Epistles to the same hand, that of John the Elder of Ephesus. Many other British scholars (R. H. Charles, E. C. Hoskyns, J. H. Moulton and W. F. Howard) have gone into the same lobby. It was therefore a surprise in 1937 when C. H. Dodd[3] joined the minority, mostly German (Holtzmann, Von Dobschütz, Windisch), who denied the common authorship.

He builds up what appears a formidable case, based on both style and doctrine. Thus (to take three of his linguistic points) some thirty words of the Gospel are wanting in the Epistle, while the Epistle has thirty-nine not in the Gospel; the Gospel contains six kinds of Aramaism, none of which occur in the Epistle; and, per contra, the Epistle has idioms (e.g. the rhetorical question) absent from the Gospel. Doctrinal differences are also present. The writer of the Epistle conceives of the Parousia, the Paraclete and the Atonement more 'primitively' than the Fourth Evangelist. Lastly, words like 'chrism' and 'seed' in the Epistle show it to be more 'Gnostic' than the Gospel.

Yet Dodd's reasons have convinced few. Instead, they have evoked a masterly reply from W. F. Howard.[4] The linguistic objections are not so weighty as might appear, and there are adequate answers to most of the doctrinal difficulties. (For example, the 'primitive' idea of the Parousia is not wholly absent from the Gospel, and the expiatory character of Christ's death is

---

[1] *The Death of Christ*, 242.   [2] *The Four Gospels*, 458ff.
[3] *Rylands Bulletin*, April, 1937.
[4] *Journal of Theological Studies*, January–April, 1947.

at least suggested in John 1.29.) In short, the numerous similarities between the Gospel and the Epistle are presumptive evidence of common authorship; and most of the differences can be explained by difference of subject-matter, class of writing, manner of composition and external situation. Dodd invites us to find the author of the Epistle in a close disciple of the Fourth Evangelist, standing to him much as a fervid Barthian to-day stands to the theologian of Basel. Most scholars, however, are with Howard in holding that the hand which penned the pastoral homily was the same as that which penned the Gospel of the Incarnate Glory.

Which came first, Gospel or Epistle? This question is still under debate; but most commentators are persuaded that some passages in the Epistle (cf. I John 2.7f. with John 13.34) imply a knowledge of the Gospel, which must therefore be prior.

It is in the understanding of the Epistle's character and its Christianity that we have made real progress in this century. Here two books must be mentioned: Robert Law's *Tests of Life* (1909) and C. H. Dodd's commentary on the Epistles (1946). One shows the Epistle to be more than a miscellany of meditations 'spiralling' round a few main themes. The other proves the doctrine of the Epistle to be at bottom common apostolic Christianity.

Law's contention is that the Epistle, closely studied, reveals clear shape and sequence. The clue to its structure is the recognition that it is an *apparatus of tests* by which its readers may assure themselves that they have eternal life (5.13). These tests are, in fact, doing righteousness, loving one another, and believing that Jesus is the Son of God, come in the flesh, sent by the Father to be the Saviour of the world. Some have found Law's analysis too neat; but a reading of his book makes it difficult to deny that the Writer of the Epistle had some such purpose in mind as Law ascribed to him. Nineteenth-century criticism often saw in I John only a rambling collection of meditations, suggesting in places signs of senility in its writer. Law proves it to be one of the most closely articulated pieces of writing in the New Testament. Besides all this, his book is a liberal education in Biblical theology in which all 'John's' main themes—God as Light, Christ as the Son of God, Sin, Atonement, Eternal Life and Eschatology—are handled with rare lucidity and grace.

In his commentary Dodd carries his study of *kerygma* and *didache* in the New Testament a step further. Their Johannine equivalents are 'the Gospel' and 'the Commandment.' And he successfully shows that, in spite of all peculiarities of thought and phrase, the Epistle by its emphasis on the Gospel and the Commandment is loyal to the Church's common tradition. The message of primitive Christianity was, first, an announcement of what God had done for men in Christ, and, second, a statement of what God requires of men who accept this news as true. It was *kerygma-cum-didache*, or Gospel-*cum*-Commandment. And in I John this original apostolic Gospel and its ethical implications are integrated completely. 'Nowhere else in the New Testament is it made more clear that the evangelical proclamation of the love of God in sending the Saviour (4.9, 14) and the commandment "Love one another" (4.11, 21) are aspects of a single and indivisible divine revelation by which the Christian religion is constituted.'[1]

I John, as Law and Dodd help us to see it, is more than an amorphous collection of spiritual aphorisms or a thinly disguised polemic against first-century theosophists. The letter takes its place in the central stream of apostolic Christianity, and becomes one more witness to a Gospel whose main affirmation is 'God so loved the world' as its divine imperative runs: 'Beloved, if God so loved us, we also ought to love one another.'

II

The last volume in the Johannine library is Revelation. 'This is a book,' said an eminent divine three centuries ago, 'which either finds a man cracked or leaves him so.' It can still do that for those who refuse the light of criticism. We have still cranks who make it their happy hunting-ground. But no one who reads a good modern book about it (e.g. E. F. Scott's *Book*

---

[1] *The Johannine Epistles*, xxxii.

of Revelation (1940)) can doubt that to-day the book with the seven seals is no longer a completely incomprehensible riddle. The scholarship of the last hundred years, especially of the first two decades of this century culminating in Charles's monumental commentary, has changed all that. After being lost for centuries, the key to Revelation has been found. What still remains dark in the book consists of 'puzzles rather than problems.'

All this is due to the discovery of two important truths: first, that Revelation is not *sui generis*; and, second, that it was written for its own time.

So many other apocalypses have turned up in the last hundred years that our book no longer appears as a Melchizedek in the world of letters. The study of these apocalypses has thrown a flood of light on the riddles of Revelation. Its literary *genre* is established; its odd arithmetic no longer puzzles us; we can catch the import of its weird symbolism.

This brings us to the second point. We have discovered the true method of interpreting it. Early fathers like Origen and Augustine, who took it allegorically, were wrong, as wrong as they were in the matter of the parables. The so-called 'Futurists,' who supposed that Revelation provided a map of the events which will precede the end of the world, were no less wrong. The true method of interpretation is known as 'Preterist.' The writer of Revelation was dealing with the events of his own time. His predictions were for the immediate future which faced him. The Seer himself declared that he was about to record what 'must shortly come to pass': at long last we are realising that we must take him at his word.

It would take much too long to chronicle all the contributions made to the literature about Revelation in the last fifty years. So far as British scholarship is concerned, we have had three excellent commentaries on the Greek text: those by H. B. Swete (1907), James Moffatt (1910) and R. H. Charles (1920). There have been other smaller commentaries designed to meet the needs of the Greek-less: Anderson Scott's Century Bible volume (1902),

Kiddle and Ross's contribution to the Moffatt New Testament Commentary (1940), and a very useful little book by Preston and Hanson in the Torch Series (S.C.M. Press, 1949). Among German commentators we need mention only Johannes Weiss (1907) and Ernst Lohmeyer (1926). And there have been many other valuable studies touching on one or other aspect of Revelation: these include:

F. C. Burkitt, *Jewish and Christian Apocalypses* (1914).
A. S. Peake, *The Revelation of John* (1919).
John Oman, *The Book of Revelation* (1923).
Austin Farrer, *The Re-birth of Images* (1949).

III

The chief matters before us in this survey are the date, authorship, composition and interpretation of the book.

The question of date needs little discussion. In the second century Irenaeus testified that the vision of the Apocalypse 'was seen not a long time ago, but almost in our own generation, at the end of the reign of Domitian.' Might it not have been written earlier, say, in Nero's reign when the Temple was still standing (cf. 11.1) or in Vespasian's reign (cf. 17.10)? After considering these possibilities, the critics are agreed, almost to a man, that Irenaeus was right. Moffatt puts the main argument clearly: 'No worship of the Emperor which is adequate to the data of the Apocalypse was enforced till Domitian's time.'[1] A date about A.D. 95 cannot be far wrong.

Who was the writer of this tract for those 'killing times' in Asia Minor? Speculations we have had in plenty, but no certainty. 'It seems,' comments Kiddle,[2] 'that the authorship of Revelation may prove the one mystery of the book which will never be revealed in this world.' The writer's name was John. But which one? For though apocalypses were often pseudonymous, nothing suggests that 'John' is a pseudonym. Conceivably he was John the Apostle, as Justin Martyr averred, if this John survived to a

[1] *Introduction to the Literature of the New Testament*, 503.
[2] *The Revelation of St. John*, xxxvi.

ripe old age in Ephesus. But few modern critics have dared to argue for apostolic authorship.[1] John the Elder, of whom Papias speaks, has had his supporters. At the end of last century Harnack confessed to 'the heresy of believing that the Gospel and the Apocalypse went back to one author.' More recently Lohmeyer has attributed both books to John the Elder who in one tradition appears as something of an apocalyptist. Resemblances of style and thought (he says) are undoubted; different subject-matter and the fact that the Gospel was originally in Aramaic while the Apocalypse was written straight into Greek will explain the rest. Lohmeyer has persuaded few, though Dibelius is prepared to find the author of Revelation in the Elder John.[2] Most scholars endorse the judgment of Dionysius of Alexandria that the grave differences of style and thought between the books preclude the idea of common authorship. We may call him simply 'John the Seer' (as Charles does, to distinguish him from the Evangelist). He was some Jewish Christian prophet of Asia Minor whose markedly Hebraistic Greek—a *Koine* unlike any Greek ever penned by mortal man—suggests that his original home may have been in Palestine. For the rest, we must be content with his own self-description—'a servant of Jesus Christ' and a prophet who 'was in the isle of Patmos for the word of God and the testimony of Jesus.'

Whence did the Seer draw the materials for his apocalypse? Much no doubt came to him, as he claims, in ecstatic visions. But the man who saw these visions had a mind saturated in the Old Testament (his book has more than five hundred O.T. allusions) and knew other apocalypses besides the apocalyptic Book of Daniel. Some of the fabric of his visions may even go back to the mythology of Babylon and Persia. (The story in Chapter 12 of the Woman, the Child and the Dragon has been styled 'an international myth.') That much of the apocalyptic imagery of the past should thus be sub-consciously reproduced in his visions, is only what we should expect:

[1] One is I. T. Beckwith (*The Apocalypse of John*, 1920).
[2] *A Fresh Approach to the New Testament*, 128f.

'Once St. Peter fell asleep in view of the quay ·of a Mediterranean seaport, whence ships were sailing to Gentile lands with live-stock for food, which perhaps he may have seen hoisted or bound in a sail. It was perfectly natural that the subsequent vision, which led to a mission to Gentiles, should reproduce the mental images which had thus come to the hungry apostle. And similarly the seer, hungering after the things of heaven to explain the things of earth, instinctively receives his vision in accordance with his previous mental imagery. But the result is something on a high plane of originality, forming a book which rightly claims to be inspired.'[1]

That diverse elements went to the making of his apocalyptic tapestries, no one denies. But other scholars have gone farther. They have suggested that the Seer took over certain of his tapestries ready-made, tapestries first woven on a Jewish loom by some apocalyptic predecessor.

Towards the end of last century the critics made many attempts to disentangle literary sources and in particular to show that the book embodies bits of older apocalyptic material. Indeed, in 1886 Vischer of Germany argued that the bulk of the book was a Jewish apocalypse (written in Hebrew before A.D. 70) which the Seer christianised by adding a prologue (1–3) and an epilogue (22) with some interpolations in the general body of the work. Even Harnack was persuaded. When he had read Vischer, 'there fell,' he said, 'as it were scales from my eyes.' But later students of the Apocalypse have not followed him. Charles, to be sure, thinks he detects the hand of 'an imbecile editor' in Revelation;[2] but elaborate dissections of the book showing sources and editors' work are no longer fashionable. The Christian elements, it is realised, are woven inextricably into the book's fabric. The impress of the same peculiar style is to be seen in every part of it. And, in sum, the modern view is that, however diverse the materials which lay to his hand, one master-mind has shaped the

[1] T. W. Crafer in Gore's *New Commentary on Holy Scripture*, 679.

[2] *Revelation* (I.C.C.), i–iv. Charles calls his hypothetical editor 'an arch heretic' and pillories his 'abysmal stupidity'!

design of this great drama of divine judgment and victory which flames to its climax in the destruction of Babylon which is Rome, and the vindication of God's people which is the Church of Christ.

To say that we are in a better position for understanding the Apocalypse than any other age since the first century is merely the naked truth. The key to Revelation is very simple, though it was lost so long. It is the realisation that the Seer's eye was primarily on his own time and world, and not on some far-distant one. Yet from what fantastic errors it delivers us! We do not need to scour the history books for monsters of iniquity the letters of whose names will add up to 666. Nero was 'the Beast,' or rather *Nero redivivus*, who (it was believed) was coming back as the Antichrist, or Devil's Messiah. But, such puzzles apart, how much other light fifty years of scholarship have shed on the dark splendours of the book! Ramsay and others have taught us much about the historical geography of the seven cities to whom the Apocalypse was first sent. Charles has not only illumined for us 'the Grammar of the Ungrammar' but has brought his great knowledge of apocalyptic in general to bear upon the problems of our Apocalypse, so that its symbols and numbers become luminous and meaningful. Researchers in the field of comparative religion have also contributed their quota. Zoroastrian *fravashis* may help us to understand 'the angels of the churches,' and the Babylonian myth of Marduk the god of light in conflict with Tiamat, the dragon of the waters, may underlie, however remotely, the cosmic struggle between good and evil, between God and the Devil, which is the Seer's central theme.

It would be wrong, however, to suggest that the problems are all solved. There remain important issues on which the experts disagree. Let us choose only two. One is the question whether in his successive cycles of visions (the seals, the trumpets and the bowls) John means us to see real advance towards the great climax, or merely repetition. It is the issue of what the pundits call recapitulation *v*. continuous narrative. Among modern commentators Kiddle votes for recapitulation: the cycles of visions are contemporaneous, parallel to one another, complementary accounts of the numerous signs which would herald the last things. Charles and Lohmeyer elect for continuous narrative: the successive episodes follow a strict sequence in time till the end is reached, and they can point in justification to such a verse as 15.1, 'the seven last plagues, for in them is *completed* the wrath of God.' The other problem is not dissimilar. It concerns the last three chapters which, as we have them, seem to contain contradictions. Has some stupid editor so rearranged them that they are now out of their correct order? Or shall we say that consistency is not to be looked for in an apocalyptist? E. F. Scott thinks we have the close of the book as John left it. But R. H. Charles has cheerfully exposed himself to the Seer's curse (22.19) by rearranging the *dénouement* of the last three chapters. The clue to the problem (he says) is that two cities are here described: (1) the millennial city (21.9–22.2) to be established on earth, where Christ will reign with his martyred saints for a thousand years; and (2) the eternal city (21.1–6, 22.3–5), lying beyond the Last Judgment and time and space, in which the redeemed will dwell with God and the Lamb in everlasting beatitude.

Hand in hand with our truer understanding of Revelation has come also a new appreciation of the Christian value of the book. So long as the key to Revelation was lost, it easily became, as it still remains with people on 'the lunatic fringe' of the religious world, a Paradise for apocalyptic 'crackpots' bent on mapping out events that are reserved secrets in the mind of God. There is no excuse for this to-day. For now we can see the book for what it really was in John's design—a message for a crisis in the Christian Church of Asia Minor at the end of the first century—and yet go on to find in it a message for our times. Moreover, though more than eighteen centuries separate us from him, we, of all generations since his day, have had cause to feel spiritual sympathy with the Seer; for we have lived through apocalyptic times when, with one catastrophe following upon another, it seemed to many that the immemorial battle between good and evil was being joined again on an even greater scale.

The amazing thing about Revelation, as indeed about most of the New Testament books, is that though their writers addressed themselves to a particular historical situation, the narrow limit of their outlook has not impaired the truth and value of what they had to say. The Seer is a notable case in point. His prognostications were not fulfilled as he expected. When he wrote, he was sure that God was going to intervene catastrophically very soon, that Christ was presently coming back on the clouds of heaven, and that with Rome's ending would come also the world's ending.

In point of historical fact, it was not the divine will that Rome should fall in red ruin at the end of the first century, and the map of history be rolled up like a scroll. The Roman Empire did not fall till three hundred years later, and history still goes on. Yet if the Seer's lurid visions of the outpouring of God's wrath on Rome were not literally fulfilled, we may surely say that his promises of divine succour for the stricken Church were realised. Nay more, we may claim that in the essential truths which he proclaimed through his apocalyptic imagery the Seer was right. Not John only but countless Christians since his day have convinced themselves of the truth of the great principles enunciated in the Apocalypse: that all history is divinely controlled; that this world is the scene of a great conflict between good and evil; that the clue to God's character and action in history is to be found in Christ 'the lamb slain from the foundation of the world'; that in the end of the day God must finally cope with evil and make an end of it; and that Heaven is the most real place of all.

The Reformers, as is well known, thought poorly of Revelation. 'My spirit cannot acquiesce in this book,' confessed Luther, and Zwingli was even more outspoken: 'It is not a book of the Bible.' Our modern understanding of it makes us value it higher than they did. The Church was right to include Revelation in its Canon. 'Sub-Christian' it may be in places; the whole Gospel may not be in it; John's distinction between black and white may be too absolute. But who that has read it sympathetically can have missed John's vivid sense of the majesty of God; his grasp of the centrality of Christ, triumphant through self-sacrifice; his conviction that in the world's battle between good and evil the Christian is called on to take sides; his faith in the final overthrow of all who oppose the cause of God in Christ; his certitude that the endurance of the saints will be finally rewarded?

IX

The Writings of the other Apostolic Men
(Acts: I Peter: Hebrews: James: Jude: II Peter)

*

I

No book of the New Testament, Harnack said, had to suffer so much in the nineteenth century at the critics' hands as the Acts of the Apostles. It suffered because the critics understood Paul and Paulinism in a one-sided way; because they formed a wrong picture of the relation between Jewish and Gentile Christianity; and because they made extreme demands—including an infallible memory—of a companion of the Apostle.

The trouble started in 1831 with the Tübingen school. Baur and others dismissed Acts as a *Tendenzschrift*; denied the Lucan authorship; and dated it in the middle of the second century. Their theory was that the Primitive Church contained two sharply opposed parties, the party of Peter and the party of Paul, and that Acts, written long afterwards, deliberately glossed over the differences between them in order to promote harmony between the two wings of the Church. Acts was the peace proposal of a Paulinist, and had small claim to be accounted history.

The heyday of the Tübingen hypothesis was about the middle of the last century. From that time on it steadily lost caste; Renan was the first to 'expose the brilliant fallacies of Tübingen'; and none did more than Lightfoot to confute Baur and his coadjutors. When he had finished his researches, it was plain that his picture of the early Church's development was much more probable than Baur's.

Then, towards the end of the last century, came Sir William

Ramsay. Approaching Acts on the assumption that it was a middle second-century fabrication, he was driven, step by step, to the conclusion that 'it must have been written in the first century and with admirable knowledge.' The spade of the arch-æologist had confounded the logic of Tübingen. With the publication of *St. Paul the Traveller* (1895) Acts began to wear a new look; and though Ramsay went too far in his claims for inerrancy, Luke's good name as a historian was vindicated.

About a decade later (1906–11) another champion of Luke arose in the person of Adolf Harnack, the greatest theological figure of his time. Harnack's trilogy on Luke's writings—*Luke the Physician* (1908), *The Acts of the Apostles* (1909) and *The Date of Acts and the Synoptic Gospels* (1911)—sought to show not only that Acts was Luke's work and excellent history, but that it was written in the Apostle Paul's lifetime. He freely admitted that in Acts St. Luke was sometimes mistaken and often careless; but his case for the Lucan authorship made a tremendous impression in this country. If some British scholars hesitated to accept his early date for Acts, they welcomed his improved version of Hobart's argument for the medical language of St. Luke. Between them, Ramsay and Harnack had struck a weighty blow for tradition.

But the Germans showed no immediate eagerness to recant their old estimate of Acts at the bidding of Harnack; and in the next great book on Acts and Primitive Christianity, Johannes Weiss's *Urchristentum* (1917),[1] the Lucan authorship was denied, and the book dated to the nineties of the first century. Yet, though Weiss found in Acts only a pale picture of Paul and Paulinism, he believed, surprisingly enough, that its picture of life and piety in the earliest days was tolerably trustworthy. English readers had to wait till 1937 for a translation of Weiss's book, and by that time it was to some extent 'dated.' But *Urchristentum* is the work of one of the great New Testament scholars of our time.

Meantime, two English scholars, Foakes Jackson and Kirsopp

[1] Eng. Tr., *The History of Primitive Christianity* (1937) .

Lake, then in Leyden, but soon to cross the Atlantic, were pro-
jecting a massive work on Acts. Between 1920 and 1933 five
volumes entitled *The Beginnings of Christianity* made their appearance. Of the team of scholars they had gathered for the work,
H. J. Cadbury and J. H. Ropes were the most notable. Volume I
dealt with prolegomena; Volume II discussed the composition
and authorship of Acts; Volume III treated of the Greek text;
Volume IV supplied a translation and commentary; and Volume
V contained supplementary notes. It is hard, and maybe unfair,
to sum up this work in a few sentences. It abounds with erudition;
almost every conceivable topic is handled with admirable fullness; but the work is vitiated by an unwarranted scepticism.
Jackson and Lake seem almost resolved to dismiss all the traditional answers to the palmary questions in Acts as unworthy of a
modern scholar's credence. To be sure, C. W. Emmet is given
the chance to state the case for Lucan authorship; but Hans
Windisch of Germany, who is briefed as the *advocatus diaboli*,
after allowing that the case for the tradition is strong, concludes
that Luke cannot be the author of Acts, because the writer had
no proper knowledge of Paul's career or his theology. The
Editors confess themselves persuaded and date the book 90–100.
On this and on many other questions these scholars seem to many
of us to marshal the evidence rightly and then to draw the wrong
conclusions; but one section of the work, Ropes on the text, is
beyond all praise.

Windisch had not to wait long for a worthy British answer.
In the final chapter of *The Four Gospels* (1924) Streeter roundly
denounced the science of Tübingen in its latest avatar. The case
for the Lucan authorship of Acts, based on tradition and buttressed
by the researches of Hawkins, Ramsay and Harnack, he pronounced 'conclusive.' The most natural explanation of the 'We
passages' (Acts 16.10–17, 20.5–16, 21.1–18, 27.1–28.16) is that the
author of Acts wishes to indicate that he himself is the authority
for that part of the history. Windisch has no right to deny the
Lucan authorship because we do not find Paulinism everywhere
in Acts. The fact that tradition names as the author of Acts one

who had himself no claim to apostolic rank is surely impressive. So Streeter argues, with his wonted power. Everything, he thinks, points to Rome as the Church for which it was written. Composed about 80, we might sub-title Acts 'the Road to Rome' and regard it as the 'first of the apologies.'

To round off this brief résumé and to show how a first-rate scholar thinks of Acts to-day, let us sum up the conclusions reached by Dr. W. L. Knox in his *Acts of the Apostles*, published in 1948.

Knox begins by refuting A. C. Clark's contention[1] that Luke and Acts are by different hands, and by deciding for the Lucan authorship. What written sources, if any, did Luke use in compiling the first half of his history? Apart from Acts 1–5.16 (where Aramaic influence is traceable) and the speeches of Peter (which Dodd has shown to represent the early *kerygma* of the Jerusalem Church) Knox finds no evidence of written sources. To the charge (levelled by Windisch and others) that, if the Council of Acts 15 is Luke's version of Paul's meeting with the 'pillars' in Gal. 2.1ff., the many discrepancies shatter our faith in Luke as historian, Knox replies that we are dealing with two separate incidents: Gal. 2.1ff. is the famine visit of Acts 11, and Galatians was written before the Council. Judge Luke in the light of what he set out to do—to describe the advance of Christianity from Jerusalem to Rome—and we must pronounce him a reliable historian. His account of the theology of the Primitive Church has every claim on our credence; and his exposition of Paul's theology ('Paul was not a Calvinist but a Hellenistic Jew') is all the more convincing 'because he does not over-emphasise that aspect of it which dominates Romans and Galatians and disappears from the rest of the Pauline Epistles.'

Now let us say something of three special problems in Acts which have engaged the attention of the experts in the last fifty years: those of the text, of the medical language of St. Luke, and of his sources.

The textual problem is posed by the remarkable readings to be

[1] In *The Acts of the Apostles* (1933).

found in Codex Bezae and its allies. Few scholars have been quite satisfied by Westcott and Hort's summary dismissal of them. The very earliness of these readings (they can be traced back to the second century) demand that we ask how they arose and whether they can possibly be original. At the end of the nineteenth century the German Blass suggested that Codex Bezae preserved Acts as Luke originally wrote it, whereas the text of the other early MSS. represented his later revision of it. Since then the controversy over the Bezan, or Western, text has raged without decisive result. Ropes, in his magistral discussion of the text (already mentioned), while thinking both the Neutral and Western texts were revisions, defended the Neutral; but in 1933 A. C. Clark, with the approval of Streeter, took the opposite view. The Neutral text is a revision; if we are to make a critical text of Acts, we must base it on the longer text of Codex Bezae and its allies. 'We agree,' says Kirsopp Lake, 'with Ropes, that both texts are revisions, but believe—as against his view—that in many cases the Western text is right.' *Sub judice lis est,* and there we must leave it.'[1]

Does the language of Luke–Acts betray the hand of 'the beloved physician'? Sixteen centuries ago Jerome spoke of 'Luke, a physician of Antioch, *as his writings indicate.*' If we could finally establish the truth of Jerome's last four words, most doubts about Lucan authorship would disappear. In 1884 Hobart believed that by discovering 400 medical terms in Luke's writings he had clinched the matter and foreclosed all discussion. Some twenty years later Harnack, while averring that Hobart had exaggerated, produced his own modified version of the argument for Luke the Physician. Then, in 1920, H. J. Cadbury submitted Harnack's case to a searching examination and dismissed the whole thing as 'an immense fallacy.' Luke's alleged medical terms could be largely paralleled in the LXX, Josephus, and non-medical writers of the time like Lucian and Plutarch. Yet it would be a mistake to think that Cadbury has completely knocked the bottom out

[1] See A. F. J. Klign's *A Survey of the Researches into the Western Text of the Gospels and Acts* (1949).

of the argument. If Hobart went too far, so does Cadbury. *Pace* Cadbury, the phrasing of such verses as Acts 9.18 and 28.8 (to take only two examples) does suggest the physician. If we do not overpress the argument, we may still use it.

It has been said that in the early decades of the present century splitting the Acts into sources was almost as popular a pastime with the critics as splitting the atom is nowadays with the scientists. And, to tell the plain truth, the scientists have been much more successful than the critics.

Since Luke used sources, including Mark, in the making of his Gospel, he doubtless also used them in making Acts. Indeed in II Acts (15.36–end) we can make probable guesses at his sources of information. Most of what he has to record came either from his own travel notes (the We passages), or St. Paul, or St. Paul's companions. It is the sources of I Acts (1–15.35), describing events before Luke came personally on the scene, which constitute the critics' 'headache.' Obviously, Luke somehow had access to the local traditions of Jerusalem, Caesarea and Antioch. Who mediated this information to him? The stories of Jerusalem can be credited to Peter, those of Caesarea to Philip the Evangelist, those of Antioch to Barnabas, Paul, or perhaps to his own researching there (if, as Eusebius says, Luke had Antiochene connexions). Nor let us forget John Mark, who must have known most of the Early Church's history. But the critics of the twentieth century have not contented themselves with speculating about Luke's possible informants. Semitic traits in I Acts have inclined them to the view that Luke had access to written sources as well as oral. And the boldest suggestion made in our times has been that of C. C. Torrey, the American scholar, who maintains that I Acts is the verbatim translation of a single Aramaic document.[1] His case rests, as in his thesis about the Gospels, on the discovery of alleged Aramaisms or Aramaic mistranslations (e.g. in Acts 2.47, where an underlying Aramaic word meaning 'greatly' has been wrongly rendered 'together'). Into this matter, even if we had the linguistic equipment, we cannot enter here. Suffice it to say

[1] C. C. Torrey, *The Composition and Date of Acts* (1916).

that experts like De Zwaan and C. H. Dodd, while refusing to go all the way with Torrey, are ready to admit that in two 'stretches' of I Acts—1–5.16 and 9.31–11.18—clear traces of Aramaic influence appear. Clearly the problem of sources in I Acts is not yet solved; but it looks as if meantime the scholars are leaning to some greatly modified form of Torrey's theory.

We may end by setting down three conclusions on which most scholars would agree.

First, Acts is the work of Luke and was written in the first century. There is no agreement about the precise date, and guesses range from 65 to 95. If we could finally agree that Luke had not read Josephus's *Antiquities* (A.D. 93) and that Luke 21 does not imply the fact of the fall of Jerusalem, the way would be open for a fairly early date. As for the Lucan authorship, we note with interest that the German Dibelius accepts it, and that though the Editors of the *Beginnings of Christianity* persist in their scepticism, few, if any, of the recent commentators on Acts deny it.

Second, Luke's primary purpose in writing Acts was not to produce some 'Tübingenesque' *eirenikon*, but to record how Christianity spread from Jerusalem to Rome, under the power of the Spirit and the leadership of St. Paul. It is also widely held that Luke had in his writing a secondary apologetic purpose—to show that the new religion was not politically dangerous and to commend it to the Roman world.

Third, the work of Ramsay and Harnack has convinced most critics that, within his limits, Luke is an honest and trustworthy historian. They do not claim for him inerrancy; they admit that in places he has been careless; they take his love of the miraculous *cum grano salis*. But they are not blind to his great merits. If it be the historian's task to 'superinduce upon events the charm of order,' then the way in which Luke has chosen his facts out of a chaos of material and so arranged them as to set forth his central theme—the expansion of Christianity to the Gentiles—is worthy of all praise. Furthermore, where we can test Luke's record by archæological exploration (e.g. local customs, official titles, details of the Roman provincial system), we find Luke faithful to the conditions of the first century. To be sure, II Acts, where Luke is writing with first-hand knowledge of what happened, ranks higher as history than I Acts; but even in those 'Scenes from Early Days,' as in the substance of the primitive preaching, we have no reason to distrust Luke as a historian; and though in places (e.g. his 'polyglot' theory of the Day of Pentecost) he may have had defective information, he has given all succeeding generations an accurate impression of how the infant Church went forth from the Upper Room, conquering and to conquer.

II

How has the First Epistle of Peter fared at the hands of the critics in the period 1900–50? The answer is that, after a period of comparative neglect,[1] this splendid little letter looks like coming into its own again. In the brief space of four years since the ending of World War II two notable books have been written about it. First came Dr. Selwyn's massive commentary in 1946. A year later Professor Beare of Toronto followed it with another.[2]

Two features of recent research are worth mentioning. The first is the theory that I Peter 1.3–4.11 is a sermon delivered to a company of newly baptised people.[3] The originator of the theory was the German, Perdelwitz. Canon Streeter and Hans Windisch gave it their *imprimatur*. And Professor Beare speaks of it as 'demonstrated.' All four, it should be noted, deny the traditional ascription of the letter to St. Peter. 'There can be no possible doubt,' says Beare, 'that "Peter" is a pseudonym.' Streeter goes even farther. His 'scientific guess' is that the author's name was Aristion of Smyrna.

The conservatively-minded reader who fears that for an authentic letter of the Apostle the critics are proposing to give

[1] In 1934, however, we had Bishop Wand's excellent *The General Epistles of St. Peter and St. Jude* (Westminster Commentaries).

[2] See also C. E. B. Cranfield's excellent brief exposition of the *First Epistle of Peter* (S.C.M. Press, 1950).

[3] This, according to Perdelwitz, was combined with a letter to a persecuted community (4.12–5.11). The introduction (1.1f.) and the *personalia* (5.12–14) are later and fictitious.

him a late and pseudonymous baptismal homily should realise that the whole hypothesis falls very far short of proof.

For his comforting, let him turn to Selwyn's commentary, where the case for Petrine authorship is put as well as it has ever been put in English. This is the second important feature in the Petrine study of the last fifty years. With Selwyn's arguments at his back, no one need be ashamed of avowing his belief that Peter stands behind this notable letter.

As is well known, on the question of authorship British and foreign scholars have long disagreed: the Germans rejecting the Petrine case almost contemptuously, the British maintaining it, often with a suspicion that their defences had been riddled.

Let us look briefly at *cons* and *pros*.

Difficulty (1) is doctrinal. The charge is that I Peter is so steeped in 'Paulinism' that Peter could not have written it. That Pauline traits should appear in the letter is not really surprising if, as we shall see, Paul's friend Silvanus had a hand in its writing. The remarkable thing is that distinctively Pauline doctrines are conspicuously absent; and where similarities exist between Paul and Peter—in the ethical sections—we seem now to have a much likelier explanation in their common use of some primitive Christian catechism at the disposal of all the early apostolic preachers. (See Carrington's *The Primitive Christian Catechism* (1945) and Essay 2 in Selwyn's commentary.)

Difficulty (2) is literary. Could an ignorant and unlettered fisherman like Peter have written the good Greek of this letter? Perhaps not, but Silvanus, who helped Peter with the writing of it (5.12), well might. The man who helped to draft the Apostolic Decree (Acts 15.22f.) and collaborated with Paul in the letters to Thessalonica, could surely have written the Greek of I Peter. In that case, the voice may well be Peter's voice, though the literary hand of I Peter may be the hand of Silvanus.

Difficulty (3) is historical. The charge is that the persecution implied in 4.12-19 necessitates a date too late for Petrine authorship and makes us think of a time like that of Pliny's correspondence with Trajan (A.D. 112) when the mere profession of the name of Christian was a crime punishable by law. But this is to read far too much into the phrasing of I Peter 4.12–19. Persecution 'for the name' was something that began in the middle of the first century; and there is nothing in I Peter which *compels* us to think of a date later than the trouble which culminated in the Neronian pogrom against the Christians.

So much for the '*cons*.' But there are several '*pros*' to be thrown into the scale of proof. Similiarities between I Peter and the speeches of Peter in Acts (the Cross as 'a tree,' Christ as 'the stone,' God as 'no respecter of persons') certainly count for something. So do the *verba Christi* woven into the texture of I Peter (e.g. 1.10–12, 4.14, 5.5). And so, finally, do certain verses which almost 'bewray' Peter's testimony as an eye-witness (1.8, 2.20–25 and 5.1, if, as Selwyn suggests, it refers to the Transfiguration).

Take it all in all, the case for tradition, on Selwyn's showing, wears a much better look than it did fifty years ago. We may with some confidence defend a date for the letter between 62–4.

On one point of detail the critics seem to have made up their minds. Near the beginning of the century Rendel Harris thought to solve the hard problem of the 'spirits in prison' passage (3.19) by introducing the antediluvian 'Enoch' and sending him to the underworld in place of Christ. The brilliance of the conjecture was too much for Moffatt and Goodspeed to resist;[1] but later commentators, almost without exception, have courteously but firmly shown 'Enoch' the door.

III

'The Epistle to the Hebrews,' declares E. F. Scott, 'is in many respects the riddle of the New Testament. Among early Christian writings it stands solitary and mysterious "without father, without mother, and without genealogy," like that of Melchizedek on whom its argument turns.'[1]

---

[1] 'It was in the Spirit that Enoch also went and preached to the imprisoned spirits' (Moffatt). The conjecture, however, is older than Harris. It goes back at least to William Bowyer, an English printer who in the eighteenth century produced a book of conjectural emendations on the Greek New Testament.

[1] *The Epistle to the Hebrews*, 1.

It is idle to pretend that in the last fifty years we have thrown much more light on it than was available to A. B. Davidson and B. F. Westcott, the authors of two admirable commentaries on Hebrews towards the close of the nineteenth century. Indeed, it is arguable that our twentieth-century commentators like Moffatt and E. F. Scott have unwittingly led us further away from the heart of the riddle.

The fact that we still talk learnedly of *Auctor ad Hebraeos* shows that we have no more certain knowledge of his identity than Origen had in the third century. 'Who wrote the Epistle to the Hebrews, God alone knows.' But 'scientific guessing' (as Streeter would say) is the critics' prerogative, and the two names which have figured most favourably in the guessing have been those of Priscilla and Apollos. To the lady, Harnack, Rendel Harris, A. S. Peake and J. A. Robertson have given their votes. Now, we do not doubt that Priscilla was a very notable woman in the Early Church: the mere fact that in four out of the six New Testament references to Aquila and Priscilla the lady's name stands first, speaks for itself. And there may be something in the contention that the suppression of *Auctor's* name was due to its being a woman's. But, at the end of the argument, we are hardly convinced, and may even have a sneaking sympathy with Hausrath's sarcastic remark that there is no evidence that Aquila was plagued with a learned wife! Those who have not given up the guessing as 'a bad job' have found Luther's suggestion of Apollos more attractive. Certainly the man whom Luke describes in Acts 18.24 —a Jewish Christian with an Alexandrian background, who was an eloquent preacher and expert in the scriptures—might well have written Hebrews. Apollos, then, or (spiritually speaking) his twin brother—this is the best guess which, lacking omniscience, we can make.

Nor are we appreciably nearer to agreement about the date. It cannot be later than 90, for Clement of Rome knew the letter. But how much earlier can we put it? 80–90 is perhaps the most favoured time; but in view of *Auctor's* complete silence about the destruction of the Holy City and its Temple—an argument from history which, writing after it, he must surely have used to support his central thesis—many recent scholars (e.g. Nairne and the two Mansons) have plumped for a date before 70.

Where did *Auctor's* readers reside? Jerusalem, Antioch and Ephesus have all had their sponsors; but twentieth-century opinion has steadily hardened in favour of Rome. It is in Rome that we first find it quoted, by Clement; and the one promising clue in the letter itself, Heb. 13.24, is most naturally interpreted, 'Those who come from Italy send you greetings.'

Moreover, if Hebrews went to Rome, it was to some group within the Christian community there that the letter was addressed: a household community, 'a little clan,' a select circle of more advanced believers.

Thus far our scholars speak with almost one voice. It is when one asks the question, What sort of Christians? that the disagreement begins. For bound up with this question is another: why did *Auctor* write them this 'word of exhortation'?

Our solution of the riddle of Hebrews depends on the answer we give to these questions. And we are faced with a choice among three.

Till near the close of the nineteenth century no one seriously doubted that *Auctor's* readers were Jewish Christians who were in grave danger of relapsing, under the stress of persecution, into Judaism. *Auctor's* steady appeal to the Old Testament, his central contention that Christianity is superior to Judaism, his fear that his readers may make themselves the accomplices of those who crucified Christ (6.6), all seemed to point in the direction of this solution. It had become almost a dogma of critical orthodoxy.

In the early years of the twentieth century the dogma seemed likely to be exploded. A group of eminent German scholars (including Jülicher and Harnack), who were soon followed by the American McGiffert and the Scottish scholars Moffatt and E. F. Scott, began to persuade us that we were totally mistaken. *Auctor's* readers (they said) were either Gentiles or were addressed without regard to their nationality; and their danger was not that of relapsing into Judaism, but of drifting into paganism.

Does not *Auctor* fear a 'falling away from the living God' (3.12)? Does he say a single word about apostasy to Judaism? Does he so much as refer to the division between Jew and Gentile? Let us put aside all argument from *Auctor's* appeal to the Old Testament, for it was the scripture of the Church as well as of the synagogue, and the second-century Apologists use it in much the same way as *Auctor*.

So they argued; and though their arguments seemed to come from the circumference rather than the centre of the letter, they laid wide open the whole problem of its character and purpose.

Now, in the middle of the twentieth century, the pendulum has swung back, though not quite to its first position. In his Baird Lecture for 1949[1] Professor William Manson of Edinburgh, after rejecting the second solution, propounds a new one which, to the present writer, promises better than either.

The clue to Hebrews is to be sought in Stephen, the true spiritual precursor of *Auctor*. Stephen's dying acclamation of Jesus as the eschatological Son of Man[2] whom 'all peoples, nations and tongues should serve' shows that he had glimpsed the more than Messianic significance of Jesus and 'the Way.' In his new eschatology and in his conviction that with Jesus the old cultus of Judaism was outmoded lay the seeds of Christianity's world-mission.[3] Here is the key to Hebrews. The Jewish Christians to whom *Auctor* wrote were not spiritually different from the men who resisted Stephen. Clinging to the ancient sanctities, they recoiled from the vision of world-mission. Hence *Auctor's* summons (in his hortatory sections) to 'the eschatological life'— to the new Exodus begun with Jesus, which brooked no looking back. Hence too his insistence, in his doctrinal passages, that with Jesus the eternal order of God has entered time and moves on to its great consummation. Hence, finally, his argument that in the

[1] Not yet published. I am dependent on published synopses of the lectures.

[2] Acts 7.56.

[3] Acts 6.13f. Cf. W. L. Knox, *Acts*, 72, 'The Living God of Israel prepared the Jewish nation so that they might be his missionaries to the whole world. This is the theme of Stephen's speech.'

new approach to God opened up by Jesus the Forerunner the old means of grace are not lost but spiritualised and perfected. To whom then did *Auctor* write his appeal? To some disaffected Jewish Christians in Rome who, fearing the Imperial persecution, shrank back under the protection of the synagogue as a *religio licita*. To these *Auctor* threw down his challenge: 'Go forth unto Jesus outside the camp (of Israel)' (Heb. 13.13).

Seen thus, Hebrews is not the *gnosis* of an Alexandrianising theologian, but an evangelist's summons to a world-mission Gospel. The letter marks 'a stage in the course of the river of Christianity as it flowed out into the great world's life.' And the date? Since the readers 'have not yet resisted unto blood,' we must place the letter before the Neronian blood-bath, perhaps about 60.

With the exception of the eleventh chapter, Hebrews is not much read nowadays. Much of the writer's grave and deep argument sounds strangely in our ears, and the relevance of his message for our times is not immediately obvious. And yet if Manson be right about the purpose of the letter, we who live in an ecumenical age may read his argument with new sympathy. In any case, *Auctor's* summons to hold fast to 'the things which cannot be shaken' should not be irrelevant for us who live in times even more troubled than his. Though his thought-forms may not be ours, we may surely hear him gladly when he sets before us the greatness of the Fact of Christ whose finished work has final significance; and the solemn seriousness with which he adjures his readers 'not to cast their confidence away' and to fix their eyes on 'the Pioneer and Perfecter of faith' while they run the race that is set before them—all this has not lost, and will never lose, its power, so long as there is a Christian Church.

IV

If Hebrews has been the riddle of the New Testament, the Epistle of James has been for centuries the 'suspect.' Origen, who first mentions it, doubts whether it is scripture. For centuries it hovered on the fringe before being admitted to the Canon. At the Reformation Luther damned it with an epithet, relegated it sans number to his New Testament appendix, and thought that it might have been written by 'some pious man who put on paper some of the sayings of the Apostles' disciples.' The letter seemed to have suffered the last indignity when, near the end of the nineteenth century, somebody wrote an article about it with the title, 'Is the Epistle of James the work of a Christian?'

Is James the brother of the Lord? Our twentieth-century scholars are very doubtful. Neither J. H. Ropes nor Martin Dibelius, our two best modern commentators on the letter, find themselves able to connect 'James the Just' with the writing. The author makes no claim to 'Founder's kin'; he makes so few references to Christ; he writes such excellent Greek. Here are three formidable objections, to start with; and there are more. Few have been convinced by J. H. Moulton's theory[1] that the letter was written to unconverted Jews by the Brother of the Lord, who, leaving out His name, hoped that Jesus' sayings quoted in the letter would win them by their own intrinsic worth. No more successful has been Burkitt's speculation[2] that our letter is 'a free Greek rendering of an original Aramaic discourse by the Lord's brother addressed to the Jewish Christians in Jerusalem.' Is then the letter pseudonymous? Ropes and Dibelius think so. But if it were so, should we not have expected some more elaborate claim to be made in the first verse? On all counts, it seems wisest with Moffatt and Hans Windisch to find the author in an unknown James who modestly calls himself 'a servant of God and of the Lord Jesus Christ,' and who (understandably enough) was later identified with the Lord's brother. He wrote, probably between A.D. 60 and 100, to some little community in Palestine.

It is in the understanding of the Epistle's literary *genre* and style that we have made progress. J. H. Ropes in his I.C.C. commentary on the letter (1916) showed that it bore many of the marks of the diatribe. His use of the rhetorical question, the dialogue

---

[1] See his commentary in Peake's *Commentary on the Bible*.
[2] In *Christian Beginnings*, 65ff.

with the imaginary interlocutor, the use of popular illustrations (like those of the rudder, the bridle, the forest-kindling spark), all suggest the style of those peripatetic preachers of the ancient world who gave us the diatribe. Martin Dibelius in 1921 took rather a different line. If we will forget the first verse (he said), count up the imperatives in the letter, and mark the morality which it inculcates, we shall see it for what it is, the finest example in the New Testament of *parenesis,* or early Christian exhortation. Much of this moral wisdom is Jewish in origin, some of it is Greek; and into it all 'James' has inserted some sayings of Jesus. In short, the Epistle of James is Christian *parenesis* cast in the style of the diatribe.

The letter is not much read nowadays, for various reasons. For one thing, it lacks the clear and authentic Christian note that keeps sounding through Hebrews and I Peter. Yet, as even Luther admitted, 'there is many a good saying in it,' and whatever he is, James is not a man of straw. His hold on the evangelical verities may seem deficient; we may regret that his letter shows so few traces of the *kerygma*, never mentions the Cross, and for an example of endurance chooses Job instead of Jesus (cf. I Peter). Yet there is something bracing and cathartic about the letter, and few of us would care to lose it from the Canon. By his stern insistence upon practice, by his healthy contempt for all shams, by his forthright condemnation of all religion which sets mere orthodoxy before a faith which flowers in lovely deeds, James provides a wholesome antidote to all evangelicalism that would save its own soul while it lets a brother go his way to perdition.

V

We may round off our survey with a brief reference to the fortunes of Jude and II Peter in the twentieth century.

Who was Jude, 'a servant of Jesus Christ and brother of James'? Our critics have returned three answers:

(*a*) The Jude of Mark 6.3,[1] i.e. the brother of Jesus and James (Wand).

[1] He seems to have died A.D. 70–80.

(b) Jude is a pseudonym (Dibelius and others).

(c) Some later Jude—perhaps the third Bishop of Jerusalem (Streeter).

(a) cannot be disproved finally, but marks of lateness in the letter (see verses 8 and 17) make it unlikely. (b) is entirely possible; but the question poses itself, Why should a later writer, casting about for an illustrious name, pick on Jude the obscure to father his writing? Streeter's guess[1] is attractive. We know that the sort of libertarian heresy implied in the letter had begun to rear its head about the beginning of the second century. Moreover, the good external evidence for the letter suggests a date not much after A.D. 100. The atmosphere of the letter, like that of St. Matthew, suggests Syria as place of origin. If, then, there is evidence (as Streeter shows there is) that near the beginning of Trajan's reign one Jude was Bishop of Jerusalem, may he not have been the writer of our letter?

This fiery little tract against certain Christian 'libertarians' at the beginning of the second century may seem to have little relevance for us. Jude does not believe in giving soft names to people who deserve hard ones. But when he has given them all sorts of 'awful warnings' from the fate of the disobedient Israelites in the Wilderness, and buttressed his prediction of impending divine punishment for them with a clear quotation from the Book of Enoch, the fulminations die away, and the letter ends with the finest doxology in the New Testament:

'Now unto him that is able to keep you from falling, and to present you faultless before the presence of his glory with exceeding joy, to the only wise God our Saviour be glory and majesty, dominion and power, both now and for ever. Amen.'

From the second century doubt has surrounded the Second Epistle of Peter; and in the twentieth our scholars, with hardly an exception, have decided that it is a pseudepigraph and the latest document in the New Testament. The case against Petrine authorship—II Peter's wholesale borrowing from Jude, his Greek

---

[1] *The Primitive Church*, 178–180.

vocabulary, his reference to Paul's Epistles as scripture, the heresy he attacks—is cumulative but decisive. II Peter is the work of one who wished to provide his letter with the prestige of apostolic authority. Its date can hardly be earlier than A.D. 150.

Some of us may wish that the Early Church had excluded II Peter from the Canon. Its authorship is pseudonymous; its Greek turgid and obscure (it is the one book in the New Testament which gains by translation[1]); and it lacks the grace and radiance of I Peter. Yet II Peter, with its allusion to the Transfiguration and its allusion to Paul's letters wherein, as the author wryly says, 'are some things hard to be understood,' has a certain literary and historical interest. Has it any other? In the twentieth century as in the second men still cry out against the apparent inactivity of God. We may or may not believe with our author that the world is going to end in fire—he is the only New Testament writer who so teaches—but, like him, we believe that some time, in a way past all our understanding, God is going to 'wind up' the historical process and make an end of evil. This being so, we may still find a message in what our author has to say to the 'scoffers': 'With the Lord one day is as a thousand years, and a thousand years as one day. The Lord is not slow about his promise as some count slowness, but is forbearing toward you, not wishing that any should perish, but that all should reach repentance.' As God is God, the Day of the Lord will come. Till then, as II Peter says, it is our duty to 'make our calling and election sure,' while, 'according to his promise, we wait for new heavens and a new earth in which righteousness dwells.'

NOTE

We have had little to say about Roman Catholic work in higher criticism. The general position of their scholars may be gathered from Ronald Knox's brief notes at the beginning of his translation of the New Testament. The first (and earliest) Gospel, written before 70, is by the Apostle Matthew, as the fourth is

[1] Clogg, *An Introduction to the New Testament*, 173.

by the Apostle John. Acts appeared about 62. Galatians is 'an urgent plea to St. Paul's converts, probably in South Galatia.' The Pastorals, which are all Paul's, appeared between 62 and 66. Hebrews is 'now accepted by the Church' as Paul's, though some suppose another hand did the actual writing. The James of the Catholic Epistle is 'the brother of the Lord,' and Peter possibly had the aid of Silvanus in writing his first Epistle not long before 67. A little later came II Peter, also the Apostle's work. The Jude who wrote the Epistle 'is commonly identified with the Judas or Thaddaeus who was one of the Twelve Apostles.' The Apocalypse is the work of the son of Zebedee.

X

The Theology of the New Testament

*

In the previous chapters we have been dealing largely with documents and their analysis, with the critical problems of authorship, provenance, date and suchlike matters, not with the religious meaning of the New Testament. But if we could recall from the unseen some scholar who had died at the turn of the century and could put in his hands some of the New Testament books appearing to-day, the thing which would make him rub his eyes would not be our opinions on this or that literary question but the tone and temper of our whole approach to the theology of the New Testament. Here there has been something of a revolution. Our scholar might be inclined to dismiss us as 'reactionaries,' but he could not but detect in our New Testament writing certain notes that were not familiar in 1900—much talk about 'revelation,' the recurrence of the word 'crisis,' the resuscitation of the word 'eschatology,' a renewed interest in the Old Testament as Christian scripture, a deep concern to stress the unity of the New Testament and indeed of the whole Bible.

We should have to tell our *revenant* that since he left the earth there had been a great revival of Biblical theology. And if he were to ask why and when this change had come, we should have to tell him something of the tragic history of the twentieth century and of the theological awakening it had produced.

For the revival of interest in the theology of the New Testament is a part of that movement of the spirit which has done so much to rehabilitate 'the Queen of the sciences.' If we had to single out a particular year for the beginning of this renascence, many of us would choose 'the apocalyptic year,' 1918, when

Karl Barth published his commentary on the Romans and by so doing threw 'his bombshell into the playground of the theologians.' The explosion of the bomb had wide repercussions. Men began to take the Bible way of looking at things with a new seriousness. And our theologians, so long preoccupied with psychology, comparative religion or the higher criticism, were driven to consider whether, after all, this really deserved the name of theology, and whether (as Barth claimed) there might not be a special revelation of God in history recorded between the covers of the Bible.

Of course, 1918 was simply the climactic year for something that had been brewing for a considerable time. The seeds of the theological revival were being sown long before this: sown in the decay of liberalism and in the whole complex of world events that culminated in the colossal human disaster of the First World War. At the beginning of the century most of us were unashamed liberals in theology. For the idea of God's revelation of Himself to man we substituted the idea of man's discovery of God. For dogmatic theology we substituted the history of dogma. We interpreted the Kingdom of God in some Kantian form of 'a Republic under the Moral Law' or as a Christian social reformer's paradise on earth; dismissed sin as humanity's growing pains; and believed in evolution and irresistible progress. In place of the apprehension of God in Christ we set the attempt to write the biography of Jesus. Not all our leaders, of course, succumbed to the temptations of the *Zeitgeist*. There were men, here and abroad —Forsyth, Denney, Kähler, Schlatter, etc.—who refused to be deceived by the so-called 'new theologies' of the time. But it needed the catastrophe of 1914–18 to show most of us of 'what strange and terrible elements the world is made,' 'how dread a laboratory of good and evil is the heart of man,' and how utterly inadequate was the Liberal creed to satisfy the desperate need of man, and to give him faith to grapple with the demonic forces in the world.

A theology so born amid the calamities of our time, so shatteringly confronted with the problem of evil, and so compelled to minister to the elemental spiritual needs of man, was bound to go back to the Bible's great ways of thinking about God and man and time and destiny, and to read it with new and graver eyes.

II

The renascence of theology in the last thirty years has brought with it a continuous flow of books about the New Testament—introductions, commentaries, lexicons, expositions, monographs on this or that New Testament topic, etc.—all of them reflecting the new theological approach to the documents of our Faith. Instead of vainly trying to chronicle them all, we propose here to pick out half a dozen books spanning those thirty years and symptomatic in one way or the other of the current trend.

Our selected six are:

Karl Barth, *Römerbrief* (1918; Eng. Tr., 1932).

Hoskyns and Davy, *The Riddle of the New Testament* (1931).

G. Kittel (editor), *Theologisches Wörterbuch zum Neuen Testament* (1933—).

Anders Nygren, *Agape and Eros* (3 vols., 1932–8).

A. G. Hebert, *The Throne of David* (1941).

O. Cullmann, *Christus und die Zeit* (1946; Eng. Tr., *Christ and Time*, 1951).

Pride of place must go to Barth's *Romans*. It is easy to say that it is most things a commentary ought not to be, that it tells us more about Karl Barth's mind than the Apostle Paul's, that it is 'an incitement to a Diocletian persecution of all historical and critical theology.' Barth himself says that it contained too much philosophy. (Besides his master, Kierkegaard, we can trace the influence of Plato and Kant.) All these charges have some truth. Yet the book remains a portent. Barth wrote to challenge and provoke; to set theologians looking at Paul in a new way; to insist that the commentators have only done the prolegomena when they render Greek words into German or English and added notes of a philological or archæological sort. To do these things is only to pave the way for genuine exegesis—which is the exposing of the Word in the words. 'I wish,' wrote Barth, 'to understand and explain the Epistle, not to provide it with a series of illustrations. Paul knows of God what most of us do not know; and his epistles enable us to know what he knew.'[1] The result was that he turned a first-century letter written in *Koine* Greek to some Christians in Nero's Rome into 'a special delivery letter from God to the twentieth century.'

Different but no less significant of the new trend was our next book, published a dozen years later, *The Riddle of the New Testament* (1931) by Sir Edwyn Hoskyns and Noel Davy. Setting out to exhibit the critical method at work on the New Testament documents, the book shows that, at bottom, the riddle of the New Testament is a theological one. Study its text, analyse the Synoptic Gospels into sources, separate up the Gospel tradition into miracles, parables, and aphorisms (as the form critics were doing)—in short, push your way back as far as you can into the tradition, and you encounter Christology—you find, in the end, not a religious genius or the last and greatest Jewish prophet, whom the Primitive Church somehow transformed into a supernatural Christ, but One who saw in His own person and work the fulfilment of the Messianic promises made by God to old Israel, who knew that with His coming the Reign of God had come and God had 'visited and redeemed his People.' Properly interpreted by historical criticism, the New Testament documents converge on a single point—an Act of the living God wrought out in the human flesh and blood of Jesus of Nazareth. In fine, the New Testament offers a concrete solution to the riddle of the world in terms of a unique Event—the coming of God's power and glory in the Life, and Death, and Resurrection of One who, 'according to the flesh,' was a first-century Jew. It claims to provide in Jesus the Messiah the revelation which solves the deepest problems of human life, as it claims also that a decision by every man concerning this revelation is urgently important.

[1] *The Epistle to the Romans*, 11.

The next notable event in the revival of Biblical theology was the appearance, two years later, of the first parts of a great new Theological Lexicon (*Theologisches Wörterbuch zum Neuen Testament*). The editor of this work, now in its fifth volume, was Gerhard Kittel (who died in 1948), supported by a brilliant team of specialists. What was new and significant in this lexicon? The twentieth century had already produced dictionaries of the New Testament—Preuschen-Bauer's *Wörterbuch* (1910; 3rd rev. ed., 1937), Abbott-Smith's *Manual Greek Lexicon of the New Testament* (1923), Moulton and Milligan's *Vocabulary* of the Greek Testament (completed in 1929 and harvesting the lexical gains of the papyri), not to speak of Souter's useful *Pocket Lexicon* (1915) and the latest edition of Liddell and Scott. Kittel's answer was that whereas these gave us 'external lexicography,' the aim of the new work was 'inner lexicography.' Without neglecting what the external lexicographers had done, the new book aimed to begin where they left off, i.e. to define the special meanings which N.T. Greek words came to possess when they were taken up by Christianity and baptised into Christ. Or, to put the same thing in other words, 'since the language of the New Testament is devoted to the one single purpose of declaring what God has done in Jesus Christ, its speech calls upon theology as well as philology to unfold its word meanings.'[1]

In each article on a key New Testament word, e.g. *euangelion*, we begin with its fortunes in Greek literature and study its use in the religious vocabulary of Hellenism; then we explore its Semitic background in the Old Testament, paying special attention to its use in the Septuagint; and, finally, we examine its meaning when it was adopted into Christianity. In other words, lexicography becomes semasiology, which is the attempt to trace the sense-development of words. This is one chief feature of the new lexicon. The other is that it is really a *theological* lexicon: it regards the New Testament as the record of a unique self-revelation of God in Christ, a revelation foreshadowed in the prophecies and promises of the Old Testament. This is only

[1] H. T. Kuist in *Interpretation*, April, 1947.

another way of saying that it bears the marks of the theological renascence and that it springs from 'a new apprehension of the original force of the Bible as the dynamic record of the creative and saving acts of God.' Some of the major articles have already been translated into English. One may hope that when the Lexicon is completed, it will all appear in an English dress. It is a rich mine for all those whose concern is with the revival of Biblical theology.

With our next book, Nygren's *Agape and Eros* (1932–8), we pass from Tübingen in Germany to Lund in Sweden. This notable work is in three volumes, but it is only Vol. I that here concerns us.[1]

When people say, as they often do, 'Christianity is love,' Nygren would interpose with, 'What do you mean by love? Is it *Eros* or *Agape*?' For in Greek these two words symbolise two utterly different attempts to solve the problem of the relation of the human to the divine. *Eros*, which is Greek, stands for man's way to God. *Agape,* which is a Hebrew idea, stands for God's way to man.

To understand *Eros*, you must go back to Plato and his *Symposium*, but it is the ground-motive of all essentially Greek religion, from the mysteries to Plotinus. *Eros* is 'the soul's sincere desire' for the heavenly; it is the *upward attraction of the soul* from the world of sense to the true and eternal world. It is primarily egocentric and human; it is the will to have and possess what it conceives to be good; and it is 'caused,' i.e. called forth by the value of its object.

To understand *Agape,* we must go back to the parables of the Prodigal Son (Luke 15) and the Labourers in the Vineyard (Matt. 20), to Paul in such passages as Rom. 5.6–10 and I Cor. 13, and to John in such passages as John 3.16 and I John 4. *Agape* is the *downward movement* of the Divine self-giving. It is primarily God's own love manifested in Christ and his sacrifice on the Cross and bearing its rich fruit in the Christian's love of his fellow men. It is free, spontaneous, 'uncaused,' indifferent to

[1] Vols. II and III deal with *Agape* and *Eros* in the history of Christian thought.

human merit; and because it loves, it creates value in that which it loves.

So Nygren draws out the meaning of these two kinds of love in a series of contrasts. The history of Christian thought, he contends, is the story (a very tangled one) of the interaction of these two different types of religion;[1] and in Augustine's conception of *caritas* we have the union of the two. Nygren thinks that *Eros* as well as *Agape* has a place in Christian theology—for at bottom they represent nature and grace—but his whole book is a warning not to let *Eros* usurp the place of *Agape*. If we will say, 'Christianity is love,' let us think *Biblically* of love; let us ever keep in mind the sheer grace of the Father in the parable of the Prodigal Son; and let us find the classical expression of *Agape* in such a text as Rom. 5.8: 'But God commendeth his own love toward us, in that while we were yet sinners, Christ died for us.'

Nygren's book set us re-thinking the Christian Faith over against Greek religion and philosophy. But a new understanding of the New Testament was bound to bring with it a new understanding of the Old, or, rather, of the Old Testament as fulfilled in the New. Of several books which have handled this problem we select A. G. Hebert's *The Throne of David* (1941) as the most brilliant example. Its sub-title—'the Fulfilment of the Old Testament in Christ and His Church'—well indicates its central theme.

In the heyday of liberalism our Old Testament scholars taught us to read the Old Testament as essentially the story of a splendid development from primitive origins. They had much to teach us that was valuable about the structure of the Old Testament and the beginnings of Hebrew religion; but the general impression they left was that it was the record of how a gifted Semitic people won through, under the leadership of the prophets, to ethical monotheism. There was little attempt to evaluate it theologically in the light of its two dominant themes, the reality of God and the Call of Israel to be His People, and to see it as

[1] Nygren maintains that the dogma of the Church expressed e.g. in the Nicene symbol is actually 'the defence of *Agape* against the efforts of an *Eros* conception to take its place.'

the record of a revelation which at last was consummated in Christ and the Church. This is the task Hebert sets himself. Defining the Messianic Hope of the Old Testament as 'the completion of the Purpose God took in hand when He called Israel to be His People,' he first describes the several elements in it—the hope of an ideal King, of a New Age, of a Divine Intervention, of a new heart and spirit, of a universal mission for Israel—and then shows how they are fulfilled and transfigured in Christ and His Church. His main thesis has been picturesquely phrased: 'Old Testament prophecies run to Christ as tidal rivers to the sea, only to feel His reflex influence upon them.' The Jews (he argues), by rejecting their Messiah, lost their status as members of Israel, while the Church is grafted on to Israel and heirs the promises made to her. So to read the Old Testament is to understand why it is Christian scripture, and not simply Jewish 'old clothes.' It is to see it as the Word of God, incomplete indeed, but finding its fulfilment in Christ. It is to regard the ancient prophecies as 'broken lights' which find their true and final meaning in the radiance of Him who is the Light of the World.

'The years A.D. 1–30,' says Barth, 'are the era of revelation and disclosure.'[1] If the Biblical theologians we have named would not all put it quite like that, all of them take the idea of revelation seriously. Now, if we do this, sooner or later we shall have to think out the whole time-process in terms of God's Act in Christ. We divide all history into two periods—B.C. and A.D. Is there not a deep significance here? Does it not call for the writing of a Christian theology of history? This task Oscar Cullmann attempts in his book, *Christus und die Zeit* (Eng. Tr., *Christ and Time*, 1951).

His book has four parts. Beginning with the Biblical idea of time, Cullmann proceeds to the 'once-for-allness' of God's Act in Christ, treats of 'sacred history' over against general history, and finally applies the salvation wrought in Christ to the individual man. The kernel of the book is its thesis that, for the Christian, time finds its centre-point in Christ. For the Greek,

[1] *The Word of God and the Word of Man*, 204.

time is a circle—a cyclic process which gets nowhere. For the men of the Bible, time is progress on a rising line, and the series of events, which the line symbolises, is controlled by the living God. For both Judaism and Christianity this time-line has three parts: (1) before Creation; (2) from the Creation to the Consummation; (3) after the Consummation. Where they place the centre makes the decisive difference between them. We may represent it, in diagram, thus:

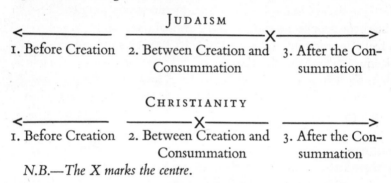

JUDAISM

1. Before Creation   2. Between Creation and   3. After the Consummation
                        Consummation   summation

CHRISTIANITY

1. Before Creation   2. Between Creation and   3. After the Consummation
                        Consummation   summation

N.B.—*The X marks the centre.*

For the Christian, the centre of history is the Christ Event. All that goes before it, leads up to it, prepares for it; all that follows it, is derived from it. For him, the once-for-all Event (the atoning Death and the Resurrection) is past; the decisive battle has been fought and won; but V-Day still waits in the future. Till it comes there will be tension. For the present, Christ reigns ('Jesus is Lord,' said the early Christians), the unseen Lord of both the Church and the world (though the world knows it not); but His is a hidden Lordship, and there is tension in the Church, which is His body, a tension not to be relaxed till the Gospel is preached to all nations and the End comes. What of the individual man in all this? By faith in Christ's work in the past, he is united to Him; in the present he is bound to his reigning Lord who sets him to work in His Church, guiding him by the Spirit; and as for the future, he looks for the resurrection of the body with a certitude resting on the fact of the Risen Christ and on his possession of the Spirit.

It is time now to pass from individual books and to characterise the main trends of this renascence of Biblical theology.

In a true sense, it has been a time of 'rediscovery'—the rediscovering of truths and emphases so long lost that they wear almost a new look. Perhaps, however, 'rediscovery' is the wrong word: we should speak rather of the Spirit of God brooding over the events of our time, and leading us to re-learn what, to our cost and hurt, we had long forgotten.

We have seen that the chief feature of the renascence has been a fresh insistence on the Bible as the record of revelation, as 'the Word from the Beyond for our human predicament,' a Word that tells of God's mighty acts in history and of His mightiest Act in Christ. If now we pick out certain trends in the theological reawakening, it is right that we should begin with Christ, in whom all centres.

First, then, we have returned to worthier ways of thinking about Jesus Christ. There has been 'a return to Christology' among the theologians. We have recovered something of the true New Testament attitude to Him, as the Person in whom God has spoken His decisive Word to us men and whose is the only name given under heaven whereby they may be saved.

It is true that the liberals believed that they were leading us back to Christ (though, significantly, they preferred the name 'Jesus')—back behind creeds and traditions and the speculations of men, to the real, the historical Jesus. It was a laudable ambition; and if they failed, there was much in the 'Back to Jesus' movement which lit up the Gospel record and made Jesus 'come alive' for men to whom He had become only a name embalmed in the Creeds. When they had done their work, one heresy at least, Docetism, seemed to have received its death-blow. After 'the quest of the historical Jesus' men could never be satisfied again with One who was not verily bone of our bone, flesh of our flesh.

But the Christ of the New Testament and of all true Christian

Faith down nineteen centuries is One who is at once human and divine. He is the God-man. The liberals gave us not the God-man, but a religious genius, all too often (as Schweitzer complained) made in their own nineteenth-century image: an infinitely noble and attractive Man who bade men learn from the lilies, took little children in His arms, spoke winsome words about God as Father and men as brothers, and died at last the bravest of martyr-deaths, only to rise to life again in the resurgent love of His disciples. But, whatever else he was, the liberal Jesus (whether of Renan or of Middleton Murry) was not the Christ of faith. He was a lay-figure not nearly big enough to explain the New Testament or nineteen centuries of Christianity. 'Why any man should have troubled to crucify the Christ of liberal Protestantism,' said William Temple, 'has always been a mystery.'[1]

It has been the task of recent Biblical theologians and scholars to recall us to worthier ways of answering the perennial question, 'What think ye of Christ?' Nor is this change to be ascribed solely to the influence of Barth and the Neo-Calvinists. It was Schweitzer who taught us that we cannot tell the Story of Jesus scientifically without talking Christologically. Now the day is past, as Vincent Taylor says, 'when anyone can be so foolish as to think that he can tell the Story of Jesus without the aid of a theology.'[2] The Liberals would have had us tell it without dogma; we have learned that this is just what cannot be done. We cannot drive a wedge between Christ and Christianity and hope to arrive at a neutral and undogmatic version of Christ in the Gospels which shall yet be historically trustworthy. At the very heart of the Gospels lies the Christological riddle; and not in John only, but in Mark also, we are confronted with a Christ who, knowing Himself to be the Son of God in a lonely sense, is not unworthy of the terrific claims which the apostolic men made for Him when they called Him 'the fullness of the Godhead bodily' and declared that in Him the Word of God had taken human flesh.

[1] *Readings in St. John's Gospel*, xxiv.

[2] *The Expository Times*, November, 1941.

It is true that in their reaction from the liberal picture of Jesus some of our theological leaders have gone too far. Statements in the works of Barth and Brunner seem to show that they have little interest in the Jesus of the Gospels—that they are solely concerned with a theology of the Word, not of the Word made flesh. Such an attitude deserves the scathing comment of Donald Baillie: 'If revelation is by the Word alone, then Christ *lived* for nothing, and the Word was made flesh in vain.'[1] In another direction, certain form critics (like Bultmann) who assert that the Gospels can tell us next to nothing about the earthly life of Jesus, go equally awry. But such scepticism (we may hope) is rare and transient, not to be taken seriously.

These aberrations apart, it remains true that one of the greatest services of the theological renascence has been to recall us to a truer view of that Christ whose figure dominates not only the Gospels, but the whole New Testament, the Christ who is alone big enough to explain historic Christianity and to redeem a lost world.

A second result of the renascence has been a return to a worthier conception of the Church and of its central place in Christian faith and practice.

Liberal Protestantism did not take the idea of the Church seriously. The nineteenth century was the age of individualism, when even pious evangelical Christians were often heard to say: 'Give us more Christianity, and less Churchianity.' The Bible might 'know nothing of solitary religion,' but many believed in the possibility of being unattached Christians. And if appeal were made to the New Testament, our scholars were ready to assert that Jesus never envisaged the formation of a new society. It had become a dogma of critical orthodoxy that Jesus never intended the Church.

We do not talk this way now. The age of individualism has given place to one that hungers for the secret of true community. When our Christian leaders meet in conference, no question is more central than that of the nature of the Church. And when

---

[1] *God was in Christ*, 54.

we pose the question, What is the Church? we are driven back to the New Testament teaching about it.

Here too the scholars have dealt roughly with the critical orthodoxies of fifty years ago. The actual word *ecclesia* may occur only twice in the Gospels, but few critics now deny that Jesus intended to create a new society. Some (like K. L. Schmidt of form-critical fame) are even prepared to defend the authenticity of Jesus' saying about the Church in Matt. 16.16. And there has been a flood of literature dealing with the New Testament doctrine of the Church.

We are realising that the Church is essentially 'the embodiment of an idea deep rooted in God's final revelation of His purpose for men, of which the Bible is the record.' And, as Newton Flew, author of one of the best books on the matter, puts it,[1] 'the conviction is growing that the need of Christian people is a fresh vision of the Church of Christ as God meant it to be, His own creation, the instrument of His age-long purpose, the reconciling Body in which all mankind might meet in a worship and service which would extend to the farthest boundaries of human life.'

Our new concern with the Church is partly due to the realisation that men must find true community or perish. This has found expression in the ecumenical movements of our time. But, apart from this realisation, the progress of New Testament studies—in particular the discovery of the true meaning of the Kingdom of God—has shown us that the idea of the Church is integral to the Christian revelation. Basically, the Church is the People of God living under the divine Rule. This Rule of God (an eschatological conception) which was the dominant theme of our Lord's preaching, implies the formation of a new community. And scholar after scholar (Gloege, Schmidt, Newton Flew and Johnston) has shown how the purpose of Jesus as revealed in the Gospels is none other than the founding of the Church. John Wick Bowman summarises the thesis of his book *The Intention of Jesus* thus:

'By direct sayings, by demands for allegiance to Himself, by

[1] *Jesus and His Church*, 13.

the calling out of a select group, the Twelve, and by the announcement of the *Haburah*, Jesus appears to have aimed at the setting
up of a definitive group in which the Kingdom ethic should find
realisation. It is concluded therefore that Jesus' intention was to
set up the Church—a fellowship of those who share the Kingdom
experience.'[1]

In fine, our New Testament savants have re-discovered that the
Church is a necessary part of God's purpose in Christ to save men.
God meant the Church—meant it to be at once the saved and the
saving community. And our systematic theologians have not been
slow to draw out the implications of this discovery.

'The idea of the Church,' writes H. H. Farmer, 'is part of the
Christian doctrine of God. The Church is not an optional adden-
dum to the Christian way of life, and, as such, something that
can be dispensed with. It is not something brought into existence
by the social instincts of humanity, a sort of Christian "get-
together" club. The divine purpose of love, in so far as it achieves
its end of bringing human persons back to the real meaning of
their life, calls into being, and must call into being, a new order
of personal relationships: it creates a new fellowship of men and
women which is both the realisation and the organ of its purpose
in history—so far as that purpose, which in the end must trans-
cend history, is realisable on the plane of history at all.'[2]

A third result of the renascence in Biblical theology has been
the re-discovery of the essential unity of the New Testament.

The American preacher, Dr. A. J. Gordon, once told an
amusing story of a conversation he had had with the deacon of a
church for coloured people. The deacon was not enthusiastic
about his minister. On being pressed to be more explicit, he
complained that his minister told too many 'antidotes' in the
pulpit. 'But,' returned Gordon, 'I thought he was a great Bible
man.' 'Well,' replied the deacon, 'he's the best man I ebber seed
to take de Bible apart, but he dunno how to put it together
again.'

Our nineteenth-century critics were not unlike this minister.

[1] *Op. cit.*, 190.   [2] *God and Man*, 143.

They were analysts. They took the Bible apart—analysed the Pentateuch and the Synoptic Gospels into their component parts, distinguished the various schools of thought in the Bible (Priestly and Prophetic, Synoptic, Johannine, Pauline and so on), laid much stress on the varieties of religious experience in it. They did not know how to put it together again. Analysis, not synthesis, was their *forte*.

It is one of the most cheering signs of the times that our scholars now see their primary task to be one of synthesis—the revealing of the essential unity of the Bible, and in particular of the New Testament. Analytical criticism, in its time, did splendid work and was of immense value for clear thinking; but it led to a piecemeal treatment of early Christian thought, and left the mind bewildered by the diversity of the New Testament. It made men propound unreal dilemmas, like 'Jesus or Paul?' It produced 'Gospel scholars' and 'Paulinists' and 'Johannine authorities,' excellent men all, but men ever in danger of not seeing the wood for the particular trees on which their gaze was focused. And it left the plain man completely perplexed by 'the varieties of New Testament religion.' Sooner or later a change of direction was bound to come—a change from the centrifugal to the centripetal. That change is now upon us. Our critics have left the circumference and are bent on the centre—on the unity that underlies the diversity.

Of this new approach we have had many examples in the last two decades. C. H. Dodd's *Apostolic Preaching* (1935) showed how the thread of the *kerygma* runs through the whole New Testament. Newton Flew's *Jesus and His Church* (1938) showed that all the New Testament writers shared certain basic convictions about the nature of the Church. Vincent Taylor's *The Atonement in New Testament Teaching* (1940) showed that, despite all varieties of approach, there was an essential unity about New Testament teaching concerning the Atonement. Floyd Filson, in his *One Lord, One Faith* (1943), showed how the religious messages of the various New Testament writers go back ultimately to the thought of Jesus. One finds the same perception of the

New Testament's essential unity in Hoskyns' *Fourth Gospel* and in Cullmann's *Christ and Time*; and the present writer, in his book, *The Unity of the New Testament*, has sought to harvest the fruits of this new approach by showing that the central theme of the New Testament is the story of salvation—a story which treats of a Saviour, a saved (and saving) people, and of the means of salvation.

All this is surely a salutary reaction from what obtained at the beginning of the century. Then we had New Testament theologies of the 'separate compartment' type which set forth *seriatim* the various theologies of the New Testament—Synoptic, Pauline, Johannine, Petrine and so on—but failed to show the constant element in them all. It was small wonder that the simple believer, confronted with such a book, was constrained to ask, 'Which particular brand of New Testament theology has the best right to be accounted Christian?' His spiritual guides gave him no thread in his hand to guide him through the labyrinth. They set Paul against Jesus, John against Mark, James against Paul. The plain man was told that the dominant theme of the Synoptic Gospels was 'the Kingdom of God,' of St. Paul 'justification by faith,' of St. John 'eternal life.' But he was given few hints that when Jesus said, 'the Kingdom of God has come,' and St. Paul 'the righteousness of God has been revealed' and St. John 'the Word was made flesh,' they were all bearing witness to one central event—the condescension of the eternal God in Jesus Christ incarnate, crucified and risen.

The plain man need be in perplexity no longer if he will listen to our modern interpreters. They are deeply concerned that he shall not miss the unity amid the diversities. They are pointing him to a common apostolic message of salvation, a common doctrine of the divine society which the preaching of that message called into being, a common attitude among all the New Testament writers to that great Act of God in the Cross which from the start was seen to be 'the hiding-place of God's power and the inspiration of all Christian praise.'

We are at the end of our journey. We have tried to trace in

broad outline the course of New Testament criticism and interpretation since 1900. On every score we have reason to write
Finis on a note of hope. The scholars of the last half-century have
not solved all the problems, linguistic, literary, historical or
theological. But in many fields there is substantial progress to
report. Textual criticism has been advanced; Aramaic origins
have been illuminated; the Synoptic problem has been solved.
The Fourth Gospel may still contain enigmas; but we have established the authenticity of most of Paul's letters, and have come to
a truer conception of Paulinism and of the man Paul. If we are
no wiser than Origen on the identity of the writer to the Hebrews,
we have solved many of the riddles of Revelation. Above all, we
have come to a new understanding of the importance of New
Testament theology, and of the New Testament documents as
witnesses to the unique intervention of the living God in Jesus
Christ for us men and for our salvation. Despite the aberrations
and excesses of individual critics, the course of New Testament
studies in the twentieth-century has been mainly to make more
sure the foundations on which our Christian faith is built, and to
increase and deepen our conviction that 'a new face has been
put upon life by the blessed thing that God did when He offered
up His only begotten Son.'

Index of Subjects

✳

Index of Authors

✳